WHEN SANTA LIVED IN IOWA

WHEN SANTA LIVED IN IOWA

SCOTT FERTICK

To my father Roscoe Fertick Jr.
and my uncle Charles Dean James.

Thank you for keeping the memory of your grandfather
E. Joy Roberts alive and sharing his message of hope with
your families and others through lives well-lived.

Contents

Introduction

The idea of writing a book about my great grandfather Earl Joy Roberts started during my winter term at Portland State University in 2002. I made the decision to return to college in 2001 to take advantage of the GI Bill earned from my prior stint in the Navy. My initial goal was to get a degree in anything for the sake of getting a degree, so I chose history as a topic that would at least be interesting. During that first fall term, however, I found I really enjoyed the discipline of history. I wrote my first research paper in a class on modern Arabia, and while I received a good grade and enjoyed the writing process, another class lit the fire that carried me through the next two years and inspired a lifelong love of reading and writing history.

The class explored the experiences of the Cherokee Nation and its dealings with the United States government. In my Modern Arabia class, the professor talked about the need for primary sources as part of the research, but more as a requirement for a decent grade. In the class about the Cherokees, the professor stressed the why of having those sources. He provided a stack of letters and documents and told me to write something, and would not, despite my pleas, tell me specifically what topic to write about. I had to figure that out on my own, which led to a deep analysis of the documents to try to find the connection. I was frustrated, but when I found the connection on my own through research and analysis, I was hooked. That was the "aha" moment when I stopped looking at history as an interesting topic and found a passion for research and learning.

That Christmas in 2001, following my first term back in college, my parents showed me a box of pictures and saved articles about Joy Roberts. For the first time, I understood the extent of his work and accomplishments. Following my experiences during the fall term, I became instantly smitten by the treasure trove of information. When the winter term began, I enrolled in a class on historiography called Historical Imagination. It was a required course for History majors and one that would have been invaluable during my first term. I learned about the history of the study of history, historians, and about the techniques and tools of the history trade. I had to write a manifesto describing what history meant to me and how I would approach the study of history.

In that manifesto, I first articulated my desire to write a book about Joy and pondered how I would go about it. Rather than trying to rehash my thoughts and feelings from over twenty years ago, I believe it is best to quote directly from the manifesto in order that the emotions and enthusiasm for the topic that existed then can best be expressed in the present. I have taken a few liberties to clean up some minor issues either ignored or overlooked by the professor and myself, but the passion for the topic is unchanged.

The last topic I want to mention is a history project I would like to work on. It came to my attention recently that my great-grandfather, E. Joy Roberts, was an upstanding citizen in his hometown of Spencer, Iowa. He was the town Santa Clause for 35 years, and had his own toy shop where he would fix up old toys and hand them out to needy kids at Christmas. His actions drew national attention at the time, and he became known as the "Spencer Santa." It is frustrating to me that I never knew the extent of his work until now. I had heard stories about him having a toy shop, but no details until a box was found in my parents' house that was a gold mine.

The box contained pictures of my father from when he was a child that he did not realize existed. The box had been moved to his house when his mother passed away years ago but never opened. When it was opened, the contents included pictures of Joy in his toy shop. More importantly there were newspaper clippings from the local paper ranging from 1917 to 1956, eight years after he had passed away, describing his work and memorials that had been set up in his honor. He was an insurance agent and a leading businessman in the community. The toys and Santa routine were voluntary.

One of the memorials for him was a tree in the city park called the "Tree of Joy" and an accompanying plaque. Out of curiosity I e-mailed the Spencer Chamber of Commerce to find out if the memorials and a children's fund set up in his name still existed. The guy who answered did not think there was a fund in his name (fortunately wrong) and said that there was still a tree but that he had not realized that it was named for a person. It was his ignorance of the topic that made me consider writing a book about Joy's life to keep his memory alive. It may be a while, but I would love to give it a shot.

My plan would be to visit Spencer to look for articles at the library from the local paper as far back as they go. In addition, I would like to find some of the articles that were written in national publications about him. More importantly, however, I would love to speak personally to people who were acquainted with him and his work. Given the time frame, they would likely be people who knew him when they were kids and may have benefited from his generosity. My uncle would to my knowledge be the only living person to have helped in the toy shop at an age when he would remember (my father was only three years old), although he lives in Alabama, and I haven't spoken to him in years. His accounts of what it was like would be priceless. I would love to write the book solely from the newspaper articles and personal testimony. I do not just want to tell the story. I want people to feel the emotion and understand the impact he had on those he touched. Not just a history, but a story that would positively impact those who read it.

The drive and motivation I felt at the time I wrote this manifesto were still there when I graduated in June of 2003. I wasted no time on my plans to visit Spencer, leaving within weeks of graduation as a graduation gift to myself. I spent a week almost exclusively in the library going through microfilms and making copies of old newspaper articles, filling a large three ring binder. While I did not interview anyone personally, I found several local history projects with transcriptions of interviews with older Spencer residents and videos of other interviews. I eventually reconnected with my uncle as well. We never had any in-depth discussions about Joy, but the memory of Joy brought our family members together for the first time in years.

Armed with everything I needed to take on the project I proceeded to do...absolutely nothing. Life has a way of getting busy. When I graduated from college in 2003, I had two children, ages three and one. I was working full time to support my family and the starving writer routine had little appeal. Two more children followed and the binder full of notes and pictures found in the box remained in the box but were always in the back of my mind. My love of history never diminished, and I soon found myself with a growing collection of books. Reading became my means of relaxing, and I read those books almost as fast as I bought them, but not quite. The challenge of reading my books became almost obsessive and other projects took a back seat to my love of reading history.

By 2024, I began to realize that my children were older, my time was shorter, and my excuses were harder to defend. I could no longer justify so much reading if reading prevented me from accomplishing my goals. The urgency to write a book about Joy started to grow, but I still had one huge obstacle to overcome. Self-doubt. Could I actually write a book that would do justice to such an amazing person? I decided I wanted to practice; first to ensure I could write a book, and secondly to get back in the writing groove so the book on Joy was not my first real attempt at serious writing in over twenty years.

To begin my new project, I went to a different box. This one contained several documents about my family and our genealogy, loosely organized, and hard to read. I decided to put that disorganized collection of information into a family history book. I absolutely loved the process of writing and the research, and self-published the book under the title *Fertig to Fertick: Following the Family Name from Germany to Jerecho*...Jerecho being my first grandchild. The book was written as a gift to my family and never intended (or likely) to make money. I liked the result though and now had instilled confidence and the belief that I could in fact succeed in writing Joy's story.

During my time in Spencer, I printed nearly two hundred pages of old articles from the various newspapers that served the city, ranging from 1898 to 1948. Those newspapers include the Spencer Clay County News (1884-1909), the Spencer Herald (1893-1915), the Spencer Reporter (1903-1935), the Spencer News-Herald (1916-1937), the Spencer Daily Reporter (started in 1935), and the Spencer Times (started in 1937). I was pleased to learn that in the years since I had gone to Spencer, the Spencer Public Library digitized their old newspaper records up to 1943 which allowed me to fill many gaps in Joy's life that I had too little time to locate while in Spencer back in 2003. Without the records kept by the library, this book would not have been possible, and I am grateful for their efforts.

While spending time in the Spencer Public Library, I had the honor of meeting another one of Spencer's most memorable and honored citizens, Dewey Readmore Books. Dewey was the resident cat at the library for several years and the topic of the 2008 bestselling book *Dewey: The Small-Town Library Cat Who Touched the World* by Vicki Myron with Bret Witter. I spent my time in Spencer rushing to collect as much information as possible and always sitting at the microfilm projector, so I never got to relax and visit Dewey as much as I would have liked as a cat lover, but he was kind enough to brush my leg from time to time as I worked and got a quick head scratch in return. Dewey's story touched many people, and the book is a lasting tribute to a valued citizen of Spencer.

The story of Joy Roberts is another story that should not be forgotten. If this book becomes nothing more than another family history book to be enjoyed by my family only, it is worth keeping the memory alive. If this book somehow manages to be available in Spencer and Clay County, Iowa, reminding residents there of the great gift they had in the person of their most generous benefactor, all the better. If somehow this story finds an even larger audience and Joy's story gains new listeners, I hope people will read his story and be inspired by his selflessness and giving spirit and maybe inspired to do their part in making the world, or their corner of it, a better place.

When Joy passed away in 1948, his friend, King Larson, sent a telegram addressed to the Chamber of Commerce in Spencer. In it he wrote, "Have just learned of the passing of my fraternal brother and friend Joy Roberts. The children of Spencer have for many years been privileged to know and love him. The children of tomorrow will be denied the blessings of his warm heart. Please extend to the family my deepest and sincere sorrow and may I join his friends and the people of Spencer in mourning the loss of the "Little Fellow" a truly big man."

He concluded with the following: "I know Spencer will perpetuate in his memory his great work." It is my hope that this book will do the same.

Share Your Fortune

❦

AMID all the happiness and joys of the merry Christmas season think of those less fortunate—of those on whom the sun of plenty has failed to shine during the past twelve months. Think of the heartaches that will be theirs on Christmas morning; think of the tear stained eyes of the little children weeping because Santa Claus could not call at their homes. Half of your pleasure at Christmas will be derived from making others happy, from sharing your good fortune and sowing seeds of kindness wherever you happen to be on Christmas day. Give something, be it ever so trifling, to the little child to whom Christmas otherwise would mean nothing. You can keep tears of sorrow from those eyes and brighten the day a hundredfold for yourself. Try it.

One

Is Santa Claus Real?

On December 17, 1913, The Spencer Herald placed an inspirational quote on their front page entitled "Share Your Fortune." While this small local newspaper from the town of Spencer, Iowa, could not have foreseen it at the time, the quote perfectly pronounced the beginning of the life work of local Spencer resident, Earl Joy Roberts. For the next 35 years, Joy would exemplify the very essence of this quote and create a legacy that is still seen and felt over one hundred years later.

"Amid all the happiness and joys of the merry Christmas season think of those less fortunate---of those on whom the sun of plenty has failed to shine during the past twelve months. Think of the heartaches that will be theirs on Christmas morning; think of the tear-stained eyes of the little children weeping because Santa Claus could not call at their homes. Half of your pleasure at Christmas will be derived from making others happy, from sharing your good fortune and sowing seeds of kindness wherever you happen to be on Christmas day. Give something, be it ever so trifling, to the little child to whom Christmas otherwise would mean nothing. You can keep tears of sorrow from those eyes and brighten the day, and hundredfold for yourself. Try it."

Joy Roberts epitomized every aspect of this quote throughout his adult life, giving freely with no expectation of returns. His drive to give and to ensure no child felt left behind and forgotten at Christmas grew from his own experiences as a child. From cold winter nights in Rocky Mountain silver mine towns, empty stockings on Christmas mornings, boarding schools, and more than his share of tragedy at an early age, Joy understood those "tear-stained eyes" the appeal to generosity spoke of. His desire to make sure no child ever felt the way he did during those lonely holidays of his youth would seem to border on obsession, but it was a selfless obsession. He embraced the well-known axiom, "Love your neighbor as yourself," but took the self out of it. He simply loved his neighbor, and the children of Spencer and surrounding Clay County, Iowa, reaped the benefits of his generosity for decades.

Over the years, local newspapers and Joy himself were all in agreement that 1913 was the first year he acted as Santa Claus. His father had passed away the year before, and his mother passed away when he was young. He got married in 1910 and he and his wife, Lena, were starting their own family. In 1913, their first child, Mary Joyce, was two and a half years old and at the age when she could start understanding and anticipating Christmas and the presents that came with it. Joy would describe it as the first year he started "playing Santa." It started quietly, providing for his family. Later in life he would recall fixing toys on his kitchen counter prior to Christmas, a habit that would grow to immense proportions for one individual over the years. In 1913, he had no helpers, and while there were no reports in the newspapers of his giving to others outside his family, he did leave some of those toys with needy kids.

1914 brought more of the same. Christmas with his family and by all accounts more giving, but still without the publicity that would follow him in the future. Joy did not crave publicity for his own benefit, but he understood its value. Over the years his ability to generate publicity and sell tickets for various local events would be unquestioned. He was a master at bringing attention to causes he believed in, and Christmas was no different. He worked throughout the year but especially around the holidays on gathering information about needy children and seeking donations to help them. By drawing others to himself and starting conversations, he created his own list of needy children that rivaled the best local charities and always had his ears open for "intelligence."

In 1915, local Spencer newspapers began to catch on to Joy's holiday activities and while the coverage was minimal that year, they were soon enthusiastically helping him with his noble cause. There were articles requesting donations, of course, but most fun for readers came from perusing one of Joy's go-to trademarks moving forward and the primary source for his Christmas lists, the always popular letters to Santa. On December 15, the Spencer Reporter made an appeal for letters not only from children, but also from adults who knew of a deserving child who might otherwise be forgotten. The letters could be addressed to Santa Claus and dropped at the local post office. Every week letters from local children were printed in the newspapers.

There initially seemed to be some hesitation to state who exactly oversaw the program (apart from Santa, of course). Readers were ensured that "others" were ready to act if the directions for sending the letters were followed, but beyond that the newspaper was not at liberty to say more. That changed the following week in the December 22 issue when the newspapers properly introduced the city's new benefactor.

The previous appeal for letters and information regarding needy families and children appeared again, as well as a request for donations to help make Christmas a merry one for those families. Readers were instructed to see Joy Roberts who would take care of the donations. The appeal included the first mention of a term that would be used heavily over the next decade. It read, "If you wish to contribute to this "goodfellowship" club and help bring Christmas cheer to the poorer folks, see Joy Roberts." Good Fellows caught on and a few years later people donating to Joy's cause would be said to have joined the Good Fellows Club, or other variations on the phrase.

1915 was also the first year Spencer erected a municipal Christmas tree, and not surprisingly, Joy played a significant role. The forty-one-foot tree towered over the intersection of Main and Fourth Streets, brightly decorated with one hundred multi-colored lights with two sixty-watt lights on top. The Commercial Club of Spencer proposed a city-wide party, with the committee in charge of planning the event consisting of Joy, J.L. Frank and John Smith. The trio did such an admirable job that the newspapers were already eagerly anticipating the potential for a similar event the following year and every year to come.

The party revolved around the children, of course, but it was a grand festival for adults too and brought in quite a few residents from the surrounding county. Over six hundred children met at the local high school and then paraded through the town double file eventually ending their procession at the tree. Santa Claus led the parade of children himself on a brightly decorated wagon pulled by four horses. The reviews did not say if Joy wore the red suit that day, and over the years it was rare for the newspapers to give credit to anyone other than Santa himself. It seems likely, as Joy played the role many times over the years, but kids did not concern themselves with such trivialities. They just knew that Santa brought holiday cheer and an abundance of treats with him in his wagon.

Over one thousand bags of candy were handed out, and Spencer High School students provided entertainment. The ladies' choir sang Holy Night, and the high school band concluded events by playing the Star-Spangled Banner, with the crowd joyfully joining in to sing the lyrics. When all was said and done, Joy had established his Christmas credentials and would soon become the city's best-known holiday personality, but some youngsters began to wonder if Joy might be something more. A few years later, the Spencer News-Herald related a story about a clerk asking a small boy what he wanted Santa to bring him for Christmas, to which the child replied, "O, gee, quit your kidding. Joy Roberts is Santa Claus." To understand how an average young man in a small Midwest town could achieve such rarefied status, we need to go back in time to determine who Santa Claus is and what kind of person one would have to be to earn that praise.

Over many centuries now, Santa Claus has been known by various names around the world, with each iteration of his evolution taking on different local flavors depending on time and place. All those variations can ultimately be traced back to the same person, Saint Nicholas. Nicholas, the real person, was born in 280 CE in the ancient city of Patara on the southern coast of what is now the modern state of Turkey. He was born to wealthy parents named Theophanes

Saint Nicholas
Alexander Donchev/
Shutterstock

and Nonna. His name, Nicholas, means "victor of the people" or alternately "hero of the people," and he lived up to that name both in life, in legend as a saint, and in his current and final imagining as Santa Claus. While the paths his life took can be followed with some accuracy, the stories that go along with those paths are glorified in the extreme, so fact and fiction can be hard to separate with any degree of certainty in some cases.

Nicholas' parents were said to be an older couple who had been unable to bear children, but after much prayer and petition they were blessed with a baby boy. This is a fairly obvious comparison to the story of Abraham and Sarah in the Bible who bore Isaac in their old age, so it could simply be the first of many religious embellishments made over the years by his admirers. Stories of his virtues and holiness even as a child abound, but for our purposes it is enough to note that his uncle and namesake, another Nicholas, served as the bishop of Patara at the time and took notice of his young nephew's potential. The older Nicholas recommended that his nephew enter a monastery to train for God's work, and once there, the younger Nicholas excelled. After he was ordained, his uncle decided to make a pilgrimage to the Holy Land, leaving Nicholas in charge of the church in Patara during his absence.

Nicholas quickly gained popularity with the church congregation and the people of Patara in general. His eventual sainthood can be attributed to stories of prayerful intercessions he made resulting in many miracles and earning him the additional moniker of Nicholas the Wonderworker. On several occasions he purportedly calmed seas and saved innocent people from persecution and death. A quick search of Google shows him to be the patron saint of sailors, travelers, children, repentant thieves, merchants, archers, unmarried people and students among others. His best-known reputation, however, was for gift giving. While serving in Patara, his parents passed away from the plague, leaving a large inheritance which he used to give generously to the poor. Probably his most famous story, and the inspiration for future legends leading to our modern version of Santa Claus, is the story of his secret giving to a poor widower while serving in Patara.

The widower in the story was a former nobleman and father of three unmarried daughters. He had fallen into hard times and was at the mercy of creditors who had already taken most of his property. The laws of the time allowed them to take his daughters as well to sell into slavery and prostitution. If his daughters were able to marry, he could save them from that unsavory fate, but he had nothing to offer as a dowry to potential husbands. Nicholas heard the story and had the means and conviction to help, but he wanted all credit and thanks to be given to God. Going out in the evening, he discreetly tossed a bag of gold through a window of the widower's residence and quickly left the scene. The generous gift allowed the widower to provide a dowry for his first daughter who married soon after.

Nicholas was not done. He returned a second time and succeeded in throwing another bag of gold through the window anonymously. With his second daughter now saved, the widower prayed a prayer of gratitude and asked God to show him "this earthly angel who preserves us from sinful perdition." Desperate to know the identity of his secret benefactor, he waited up one evening and as expected, another bag of gold was thrown through the window. His daughter had left some stockings by the fire to dry, and the gold landed in a stocking, or in alternative versions, in a pair of shoes. The widower pounced at the opportunity and caught up to Nicholas before he could leave the area. He thanked Nicholas profusely, but true to his intentions, Nicholas told him to keep the source of the gold a secret and give all the glory to God.

After a few years serving the church in Patara, Nicholas sought to go on a pilgrimage to the Holy Land like his uncle had before him. He stopped in Alexandria and then Jerusalem, always ministering to those he met on the way. It was passed down that when he entered churches at various holy sites, the doors would open on their own to allow him in, such was his great holiness. Upon leaving the Holy Land, he returned to his home country and spent time at the Monastery of Holy Sion. He considered retiring permanently to the monastery but felt he still had much to offer to his people and his congregation. Instead of returning to Patara, however, he relocated to the larger coastal city of Myra where he would live for the rest of his life serving as an archbishop.

Between 302 and 313 CE a collection of Roman emperors attempted to suppress Christianity through imprisonment and persecution, with astounding levels of cruelty towards clergy and at times against entire towns. Nicholas did not cave in to the threats and ended up in prison for several years. He persevered, however, and when Constantine rose to power and converted to Christianity, Nicholas and many other prisoners were released. He used his newfound freedom and the blessings of the emperor to become a champion in the fight against paganism. In 325 CE, Constantine ordered the Council of Nicaea to convene in the hope of combating perceived heresies that had arisen and setting common standards to be followed throughout the church. Nicholas was an active and outspoken participant, even getting himself in a bit of trouble when he struck the heretic Arius, although he was quickly forgiven.

Nicholas continued to faithfully serve the church in Myra for many years before passing away on December 6, 343 CE. As is common with legends, and more so with saints, stories of his life, miracles and generosity were embellished even more upon his death. Thousands of churches have borne his name in the past and through the present. Of all his accomplishments, the tradition of secret gift giving has endured the most, even among those who no longer recognize who or what inspired their acts of kindness. It became tradition to give gifts on the anniversary of his death, often in shoes or stockings in memory of his giving to the poor widower and his daughters.

Over the centuries, the legend of Saint Nicholas grew, spreading west into Europe and north into Russia, where in 988 CE, Vladimir the Great made him the patron saint of his entire country. In time, the legend arose that it was Saint Nicholas himself who would visit on the eve of December 6 to deliver treats to good children and to punish the bad. In some countries, rumor had it that he rode on a white horse, but in Russia and other northern countries where horses were rare or non-existent, the tradition spread that he would use reindeer as his preferred mode of transport. At this point it is easy to see where many of our current traditions had their beginning, but there were still many twists and turns to come. Several changes happened when church traditions were put under scrutiny during the period of the Reformation.

During the early 16th century, Martin Luther in Germany and King Henry VIII in England wanted to do away with the worship of and praying to saints. Both understood the value of traditions, however, so they strived to alter the focus of the traditions surrounding the holidays. Luther for his part, taught that Christ was the true giver of gifts, not any saint, so he sought to focus the Christmas traditions on the Christ Child, or in German, Kris Kindl. This eventually morphed into the familiar Kris Kringle. King Henry VIII had motivations that were not quite as noble. He left the Roman church and created the Church of England so he could divorce his wife. To sway the newly formed congregations away from saint worship, he created the persona of Father Christmas and instead of a feast day reminiscing the death of Saint Nicholas, moved the feast to Christmas Day.

Adding to the new image of Father Christmas, the priestly garments worn by Saint Nicholas were replaced by thick, colorful robes; sometimes red and sometimes green. By now, the tradition of a benevolent soul bringing presents and treats on Christmas seemed fairly settled, but the appearance and personality of that benefactor would still go through several variations and eventually make it across the Atlantic Ocean to the New World. It was not, as some would think, the Pilgrims who brought the stories with them. As Puritans, they wanted to break away from the Church of England and did not celebrate Christmas at all. The first stories of Sant Niklaas to come to America were from the Dutch who settled in New Amsterdam, the island that would eventually become Manhattan. When the island changed into British hands, new settlers from England brought the Father Christmas traditions with them and the two personalities began to merge into the Santa Claus we know today.

The first American contribution to the evolving Christmas traditions came from Washington Irving, best known for writing The Legend of Sleepy Hollow and Rip Van Winkle. In 1809 he wrote the satirical A History of New York under the pseudonym Diedrich Knickerbocker who was a made-up Dutch historian. In this history of the Dutch presence in what would become New York, one of the characters described Saint Nicholas in traditional Dutch clothing flying over the rooftops in a horse drawn wagon with a large pack of toys to distribute specifically to children. He would enter the homes of his favorites, presumably the well-behaved children, by going down the chimney and filling their waiting stockings. Irving's descriptions of Saint Nicholas would have a significant influence on the next big step in Santa's progression fourteen years later, including the peculiar habit of "laying his finger beside his nose" before flying off to the next house.

The "finger aside his nose" showed up again in one of the best-known poems in American history, and one of the most influential. In 1823, the Reverend Clement Clarke Moore wrote "A Visit From St. Nicholas" for his family, and many now know it as The Night Before Christmas. From the fur-lined coat to the pack of toys, to his rosy cheeks and his belly "like a bowl full of jelly," most people can easily recognize if not accurately quote most of the descriptions provided in the poem. While borrowing heavily from Washington Irving, Moore reintroduced the idea of a sleigh drawn by reindeer and had his "jolly old elf" visit on Christmas Eve, not Christmas Day, and both changes are still the accepted norm to this day. The impact of the poem on Christmas traditions and the idea of gift giving was immediate and lasting. As magical as the written imagining of Saint Nicholas was to the American public, forty years later a political cartoonist would provide visual images that captured the public's attention once again and started to solidify the look that would be so familiar to Joy Roberts when he began playing the role of Spencer's Santa.

Thomas Nast is generally credited with creating the modern version of Santa Claus. Writing for Harper's Weekly, Nast produced thirty-three drawings of Santa between 1863 and 1886. His early sketches, drawn during the Civil War, showed that the jolly old saint had an unquestioned loyalty to the Union cause. His first drawing, published on January 3, 1863, showed Santa distributing gifts to Union soldiers while wearing a blue coat covered in stars and red and white striped pants. Most of his Civil War era sketches are easily recognizable as propaganda, true to his political cartoonist roots. Even after the war, many of his sketches continued to show support for soldiers and the various causes they espoused, including better pay and treatment in the 1880s. Whatever his subtle messaging may have been, it was the image of Santa Claus that caught America's attention.

Nast's version of Santa Claus evolved over time from a smaller elfish character to the full size and decidedly more rotund vision of today. He took some queues from Moore's poem for his background scenes and even modeled some characteristics on himself such as his beard and ample belly. His 1881 portrait entitled "Merry Old Santa Claus" is easily recognizable today and probably the best-known image of Santa created by Nast. There are elements of propaganda in the toys he is holding to those familiar with the day's current events, but the depiction of Santa is where the lasting impact was most profound. The drawings of Nast appear to have impacted Santa's first known appearance in an adver-

Merry Old Santa Claus by Thomas Nast

tising campaign. In 1868, the US Confection Company used Santa Claus to advertise sugar plums, complete with red suit and white whiskers, riding in a sleigh pulled by multiple reindeer.

These are the images that would have been familiar to Joy during his childhood and as he created his own holiday persona. Coca Cola is often assumed to have created the modern version of Santa Claus during their 1930s advertising campaign, but their Santa was influenced by Thomas Nast. Joy would have likely

1861 sugar plum advertisement
featuring Santa Claus
Library of Congress

been familiar with stories attributed to Santa in Frank Baum's *Life and Adventures of Santa Claus*, published in 1902, two years after he published *The Wizard of Oz*. How much those stories influenced Joy is not known, but over the years he developed his own ideas on how to play the part. He was very careful about how he looked when portraying Santa, keeping his fake whiskers tight against the inevitable tugs of children. He did not bother with the big belly. Joy was a small, thin man and worried that a poke in the false paunch would be a dead giveaway for inquisitive children. Joy wanted children to believe in Santa Claus and believe with all their heart.

This brings us to the big question...is Santa Claus real? One would be hard pressed to convince children around the world that there is no such person. Whether he is the Santa Claus most of us know, or any other iteration from various cultures, children who are lucky enough to enjoy Christmas believe religiously that there is a generous soul out there somewhere who cares for them and will bring them joy during the holidays. The debate over whether Santa is real is a debate for children, and one they should be allowed to have while their hearts are still open to the possibility. Joy's advice to parents regarding what to tell children about Santa was simple. "Let them make up their own minds." Children will eventually move away from believing Santa is a real person in almost all cases, but why rush it and take away one of the great mysteries of childhood?

But what about us adults? What are we to believe about Santa Claus? It would be a challenge to find an adult who believes Santa is a real person, and even more so to find one that admits it if they do. As we get older, we are fond of speaking of the spirit of Christmas instead, and by that we usually mean a spirit of giving. Giving is the true heart of Christmas. Those who take the most joy during the holidays from giving have that spirit. Those whose only joy from Christmas is from what they receive, quite frankly, do not have that spirit. I believe we can all make an exception for children in this case. The spirit of giving in us is at its height when we give to children and see the joy they receive from our efforts on their part.

If we forgo the possibility of Santa being a real person, we need to change our line of thought towards the spirit of Christmas, and in doing so we may find more truth than we expect. I am inclined to believe that Santa Claus epitomizes the spirit of Christmas...of giving...so if the spirit of Christmas is real, so is Santa Claus. The spirit of Christmas rests on all of us around the holiday, if we are fortunate. Some feel it more than others and the best of us act on those impulses, giving generously and enthusiastically to the best of our ability. Then there are those who have the spirit of giving year-round. Joy was one of those. To put better words than mine to this thought, we have to go no further than Joy's wife, Lena, for explanation.

Following that first municipal Christmas in Spencer in 1915, Joy and Lena welcomed their second child, Charles, in May of 1916. Charles and his sister Joyce grew up like most children believing wholeheartedly in Santa Claus. They also grew up watching Joy distribute toys at

----

Come Down Chimney

Dear Santa Claus,

I have tried to be a very good boy this year. I wish you would come down my chimney and bring me a train, a book, a steam engine and a foot-ball.

A Merry Christmas for dear Santa and all his helpers.

Your friend,
Charles Roberts

A letter to Santa Claus from young Charles Roberts

The Spencer News-Herald

Christmas and even helped him repair old toys for that very purpose. Later in life, Joy shared the story with a reporter about the day when Charles began to have his doubts. He was twelve years old when he asked Joy if there really was a Santa Claus, and true to his advice to other parents, Joy asked him what he thought. Charles went to his mother to discuss the question, and her advice to him shows perfectly how children, and maybe even some adults, could believe that Joy was in fact Santa Claus.

"Santa means many things to many people. To some folks, he's just a funny fellow who puts tangerines and mouth harps in children's stockings. To those folks, it doesn't make much difference whether Santa really exists or not. But when Santa leaves behind gifts of love and affection—then folks have to admit somebody special has been around, and you can call him Santa Claus, or Kris Kringle, or Saint Nick, or any one of a dozen names. In this case, you might call him Joy Roberts."

Two

Just Had to Grow Out of It

The decision Joy Roberts made to dedicate his life to making children happy on Christmas was born of experience. He had a transient childhood and suffered more than his share of loss by the age of twelve. He grew up in a mining camp in Leadville, Colorado where possessions were sparse. He lost his mother at a young age and soon afterwards his father took him to Tennessee where he spent his formative years living in boarding schools. Later in life he appeared somewhat stoic regarding his difficult early years, telling a reporter in 1947, "I guess I just had to grow out of it." He did grow out of it, but he always remembered.

Joy understood the holiday season can be a difficult time for people. Those whose lives are difficult on the best of days seem to feel it even more around Christmas. Life for most of us seems happier, merrier if you will, in December with the joy of the season, the anticipation of gifts to be given and received, and the closeness of family. For those who go without or feel left out, the happiness of others can drive home the hopelessness of their own deficit. For children, memories of Christmas without Santa Claus, without gifts, and without hope can last well into adulthood. Joy could relate to those feelings of loss. "I've seen Christmases where I didn't get a thing," he said, "so I know what it's like."

When Joy reached adulthood and began his role as Spencer's Santa Claus, he settled into Clay County life and never left. The involuntary wanderings of his childhood ceased, and he chose a stationary life for himself and his family. He never confirmed publicly if that was a conscious decision to compensate for the unsettled nature of his youth. The constant movement and unfortunate tragedies he endured in no way indicated an unhappy family life. By all accounts his parents were good people. His mother, Mary Roberts, was said to be a "woman of many good qualities." His father, Thomas Roberts, had a cheerful personality which led to him being affectionately referred to in Spencer as "Uncle Tommy." He was, however, a wanderer if his life is any indication, so it is with his life that we will begin to explore Joy's youth in more detail.

Thomas Lynn Roberts was born in South Wales on June 13, 1837, to Philip and Mary Roberts. Mary Roberts was the daughter of Louis and Elizabeth Lewis. Elizabeth, Thomas' grandmother, lived to the astonishing age of 111 years old. The Lewis family provides some curious uncertainties regarding their family history. Louis and Elizabeth had four daughters and one son. One of the daughters married Morgan Howells, a well-known Methodist minister in his day, making him Thomas' uncle. Morgan Howells had a brother-in-law named Richard Lewis, or more popularly, Dic Penderyn, a character, either famous or infamous in Welsh history depending on a person's perspective.

Dic Penderyn is well known in Wales as a working-class martyr falsely accused (allegedly) of injuring a British soldier during the riots of 1831 and hanged as an example. He may have been the one son of Louis and Elizabeth Lewis and Mary Roberts' brother, but due to poor records and the preponderance of people with the last name of Roberts or Lewis in Wales at the time, the exact connection may never be known. Morgan Howells married twice in his lifetime, his first wife dying relatively young, and there is a lot of confusion among even professional historians regarding Dic Penderyn's family. Which wife of Morgan Howells was Dic's sister and whether Dic was Thomas' uncle will be left to others to debate for now.

Thomas was three years old when his parents moved to America and settled in Minersville, Pennsylvania. He grew to adulthood in Minersville, attending public schools and learning the machinist's trade. In 1860, he and his parents relocated to Columbus County, Wisconsin. One year later, following the outbreak of the Civil War, he joined Company C of the Twelfth Wisconsin Volunteer Infantry, enthusiastically embracing the Union cause. He spent the first three years of his service as a drummer boy before reenlisting in 1864 while in Vicksburg, Mississippi, as a private working in the quartermaster's department. He took part in several battles while marching from Vicksburg to Atlanta and joined General Sherman on his famous march to the sea.

After the war, Thomas returned to Wisconsin for two years working as a clerk in a department store. While in Wisconsin, he married Mary Ann Richards, the daughter of Hugh and Anna Richards. Mary was born on May 12, 1846, in Utica, New York. She and Thomas had five children together over a period of twenty-one years, starting with Adelbert Studer Roberts in 1867 and ending with Earl Joy Roberts in 1888. The birth of their first child marked the beginning of a transient lifestyle for the Roberts family that continued until well after Joy was born, so tracking the family history can be a bit of an adventure. Ultimately the goal is to follow Joy's life, but an attempt will be made to summarize the family movements leading up to his birth.

MR. AND MRS. T. L. ROBERTS
History of Clay County

Adelbert, who went by Bert, was born in Wisconsin in 1867. Shortly thereafter, the family moved to Omaha, Nebraska where Thomas returned to the machinist trade he learned while growing up in Pennsylvania. He started working for Union Pacific Railroad putting in line shafting, and his biography claims he installed the first air pump ever on an engine west of the Missouri River. During their time in Nebraska, Thomas and Mary had a second child named May. The best guess on her date of birth would be in January of 1870. May passed away when she was three and a half years old. Prior to her passing, a third child was born. Thomas Lynn Roberts Jr was born on January 23, 1872, not in Nebraska, but at a place called Trimello in Clay County, Iowa.

Thomas Jr's birth in Iowa makes sense as his father invested in land in Clay County around that time. In 1870, Thomas Sr had been given 160 acres in Spencer on a soldier's claim. He made a solid investment, as he paid only $16 and by the time his biography was recorded around 1908 the value of the land had increased to $12,000. What exactly is a soldier's claim? In 1862, President Abraham Lincoln signed the Homestead Act of 1862 to encourage expansion and settlement to the West by offering free land. The requirements stated that an individual must be at least 21 years old, head of a household, and never have taken up arms against the government. To keep the land, the homesteader agreed to reside on the land and improve it for five years, after which they would become the sole owner of the land for free, minus the filing fee, which appears to have been the $16 paid by Thomas.

There were a few extra perks added for Civil War veterans. The age requirement could be waived for veterans under 21 years of age. After the war, veterans could also deduct the number of years they served from the five-year residency requirement. That would have applied to Thomas' four years of service, so he was able to keep the claim despite moving away from Iowa again in 1873. After a few years of cultivating his new claim he returned to the machinist trade, this time moving to Rawlings Springs, Wyoming, to work for the Rio Grande Railroad Company. He would return to Iowa from time to time and leave his wife there on occasion. Her obituary says she spent most of her married life in Colorado and Wyoming though, so for the most part the family stayed together when they could.

Sometime in the late 1870s, the family moved from Wyoming to Leadville, Colorado, where Joy would eventually be born. Leadville was first settled by gold miners around 1860. The area was remote and located over ten thousand feet above sea level. When it looked like the gold would eventually run out, silver deposits were discovered, and the Colorado Silver Boom began. Leadville, despite being a classic example of the wild, wild west, prospered, becoming at one point the second largest city in Colorado behind Denver. The city was officially founded in 1877 around the same time the Roberts family arrived, following the railroads that were needed to move the town's bounty.

State Street in Leadville during the early 1880s
George D. Wakley

The first couple of years the Roberts family spent in Leadville may have been precarious at times as the population exploded from three hundred in 1877 to 15,000 in 1878 and the new city developed a reputation for lawlessness. The first sheriff got run out of town, and his replacement was shot by one of his own deputies after only one month on the job. Desperate, the mayor hired Mart Duggan, a gunfighter with a reputation for questionable but effective tactics. Duggan brought needed law and order to Leadville and stepped down in 1880. He was not the only well-known gunfighter to spend time in Leadville over the years. Doc Holiday came to town in 1882 and worked as a faro dealer. In 1884, he shot Billy Allen over a gambling debt. Allen lived, but Holiday went on trial for attempted murder. A jury acquitted him despite the evidence thanks to a combination of laws on self-defense, and maybe in part to his fame.

While living in Leadville, Thomas and Mary had two more children. Patrina May was born around 1880. Joy, the youngest, followed eight years later, on July 19, 1888. During the 1880s life for the family probably mirrored that of the city which grew very prosperous at the time. One success story to come out of Leadville was Maggie Tobin, who moved to Leadville when just eighteen years old in 1885. She lived in poverty and married an equally poor gentleman named James Joseph Brown. The family struck it rich in 1893, but the pressures of wealth and society led to their eventual separation. Maggie Brown was financially secure, however, thanks to a generous agreement following the divorce. In 1912, she survived the sinking of the HMS Titanic, and in time gained fame as the Unsinkable Molly Brown.

There were many success stories from Leadville in the early days, and the Roberts family may have shared that success on a smaller scale. Like many boom towns, however, the bust was never far away. For both the family and the city, the 1890s were devastating. Sometime around 1891, Thomas and Mary lost another daughter when Patrina passed away at the age of eleven. Only three years old at the time, Joy may not have fully grasped the loss, but it was only the first of three family tragedies in the decade. For the city of Leadville, prosperity ended in 1893 with the passage of laws that caused the price of silver to plummet and the city slowly lost its relevance.

When Joy and his family returned home to Spencer, Iowa, is not entirely clear. Family members may have moved at different times leading to the feelings of chaos in his youth that Joy lamented occasionally as an adult. Various reports show Joy moving back to Spencer when he was four or five years old. There may have been more wandering back and forth over the years. Joy himself talked of memories from Leadville when he was nine years old, in 1897, that played a major role in his later desire to help kids in need. He recalled hanging stockings on Christmas Eve, only to find them empty on Christmas morning. Nearly fifty years later, he remained very resolute, stating, "Since then I've made up my mind that no kids around me were going to have that if I could help it." It would seem Joy and his family suffered from the effects of Leadville's decline like many others.

By the end of 1897 at the latest, Joy left Leadville behind and returned to Spencer. The first two years back, however, were some of the most tragic of his young life and ultimately led to more wandering during his teenage years. Right before Christmas in 1897, Joy's mother, Mary, fell ill and was diagnosed with cancer. In January his brother Thomas Jr moved back to Spencer from Leadville with his wife, Haidee, probably in response to his mother's illness. In early March, Mary traveled to a hospital in Chicago, but the doctors could do nothing for her. She passed away in Chicago on March 18. The family brought her body back to Spencer and buried her in a family plot at the local cemetery.

The loss of a mother is difficult for any child, of course. If there was a bright spot, it may have been that just three weeks prior to his mother's death, Joy had become an uncle. His brother Thomas Jr and his wife welcomed their first son, Maryan, on February 28, 1898, soon after their return to Spencer. The new life may have been a comfort during the loss of another, but unfortunately more tragedy was to come for the young family and for Joy. On September 20, 1899, Thomas Jr was killed in a train accident in Windom, Minnesota, leaving behind his wife and young son.

Thomas Jr would have been raised around trains growing up with his father working for various railroad companies, and he followed his father in that trade. He worked as the fireman on a freight train making a run from Sioux City, Iowa, to St. James,

Minnesota. The train carried a heavy load requiring two engines. They were approaching Windom at full speed, and as the train came around a hill leading to a bridge across the Des Moines River, they realized too late that another train had stalled ahead with its back end still on the bridge. The stalled train had an engine attached to its rear, so the three engines collided in the middle of the bridge and all three, along with twenty-five loaded cars, collapsed with the bridge into the river below. While some of the crews were able to jump clear, Thomas Jr and his engineer went down with the wreck.

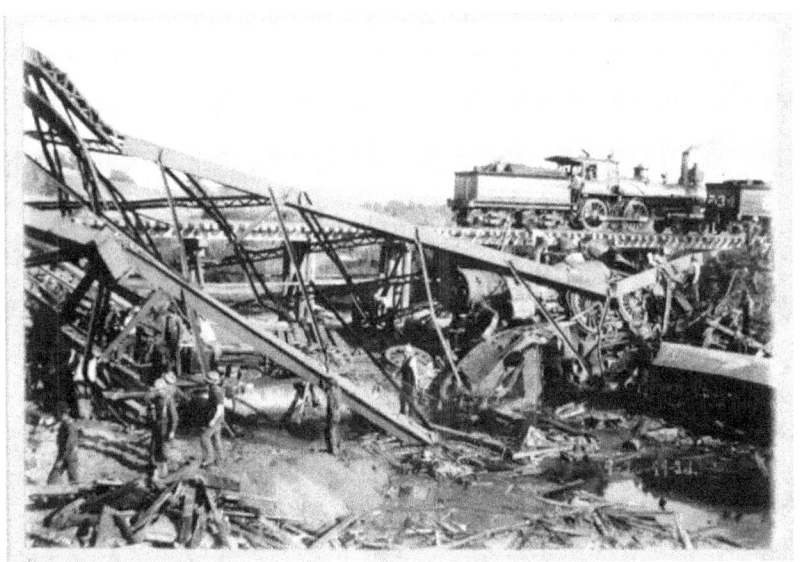

Train wreck that took the life of Thomas Roberts Jr. in 1899
Cottonwood County Historical Society

Pictures of the wreckage show a tangled mess of metal one would expect following such a chaotic scene. Thomas Sr had been visiting friends in Madison, Wisconsin, and after a brief return to Spencer left for Windom to help in the search for Thomas Jr and the engineer. It took several days to find them, but the body of Thomas Jr was located and returned to Spencer where he was laid to rest near his mother on October 2. The following year, for reasons never made clear, Thomas Sr and Joy moved to Tennessee. It may have been a needed change of scenery, but it marked a continuation of the odyssey that defined Joy's youth.

Later in life, when Joy talked about being raised in boarding schools, he appeared to be referring to his time in Tennessee. There is not a lot of specific information about his first couple of years there when he would have been twelve years old, but the obituaries of both Joy and Thomas indicate they were separated during that time. Thomas settled in the Somerville area near Memphis while Joy spent his school years near Nashville over one hundred miles away. There may have been other schools, but the only schools we have record of for Joy were Dixon Preparatory School and Vanderbilt University, where Joy had earned a football scholarship. The records are scarce and future newspaper articles occasionally differed on specifics, so a best guess will have to do regarding those years.

Dixon Prep, as the local Spencer newspapers referred to it, was a school located in Dickson (not Dixon), Tennessee. Dickson Academy had been established in Dickson during the mid-1880s around the same time that a new college started up in the western part of Dickson County called Edgewood Normal School. Edgewood began operations as a small schoolhouse and grew into a new college. "Normal" schools sound odd nowadays, but the term referred to schools designed to prepare students for careers in education. The Edgewood school eventually purchased the Dickson Academy property, and the professors established Dickson Normal School which quickly became one of the top colleges in the state, comparable to Vanderbilt and the University of Tennessee.

Postcard of Dickson College

Dickson College operated as a private school and remained open until 1912, at which time it was shut out of funding in favor of public schools and closed. Joy probably attended between 1906 and 1910, possibly earlier as a boarding student. Local newspapers in Spencer loved the idea that Joy earned his way through college on a football scholarship. He only weighed around 145 pounds and was one of the smaller college players in the country. He played end, the equivalent at the time of a wide receiver today. According to future articles which varied in their reports, he either played all four years at Vanderbilt, or spent three years at Dickson College and one year at Vanderbilt. He is not mentioned on the rosters listed in the yearbooks from Vanderbilt during those years, so there is another scenario that might make sense.

In the early 1900s, Dickson College fielded its own football team. Nicknamed the "Maroons" for the color of their jerseys, the team played several years before disbanding. It seems likely that Joy's scholarship days were spent on the gridiron in Dickson, at least for the first three years. The year at Vanderbilt is in question based on his lack of acknowledgment on their rosters, but there is another possibility. After Joy had extinguished his college football eligibility at Dickson, he attended medical school at Vanderbilt, but without the scholarship he was unable to continue his education due to lack of funding. Specifics being evasive, what we do know is that after leaving college he returned to Spencer in 1910.

By the time Joy came home to Spencer, Thomas had already returned. In 1908, Thomas' biography was included in a book called *History of Clay County,* which labeled him a representative citizen of Spencer. He still owned his homestead claim but had retired. His "life of activity and enterprise" provided him with "all the comforts and some of the luxuries of life without recourse of further labor." Joy never mentioned what happened to the land or any money that eventually came from it. From the sound of it, Thomas may have sold the land and lived his final years on the proceeds. Any money left may have gone to Joy and his brother Bert. Over the years Joy used his own money to fund his Christmas giving when contributions were short, so any long-term benefit likely went to the needy children of Spencer.

When Joy returned to Clay County, he lived in nearby Estherville working as a store clerk, ready to make his own way in life. Soon thereafter, he married and settled down in Spencer, his life of constant displacement left behind for good. On May 8, 1910, Joy married Lena Moorehouse at her mother's house in Spencer. Lena was born in Spencer on March 10, 1885. She was the daughter of Charles and Lucy Moorehouse. She lived her entire life in Northwest Iowa where she graduated from Spencer High School and attended Western Union College in LeMars. At the time of their marriage, she worked as a teacher in Spencer. Just under a year after their marriage, Joy and Lena welcomed their first child, Mary Joyce Roberts, on April 22, 1911.

Lena would be the perfect complement to Joy...Mrs. Claus to his Santa. Over the years Santa would occasionally make appearances in Spencer with Mrs. Claus at his side. On the occasions when Joy played Santa, she may well have been there playing the part with him, but no specific reports confirm it. She stayed active in many women's groups in Clay County and had her own causes to support, but her most generous contribution to Joy may have been her tolerance. Joy would eventually receive so much support in his work, especially when it came to collecting toys for the children of Spencer, that the toys slowly took over the kitchen counter, then the garage and other rooms. Later in life the bigger toys were kept on the front porch because they had no more room in the house, much to the delight of neighborhood kids who would stare at Santa's house with wide-eyed wonder.

On August 17, 1912, Joy's father, Thomas Sr. passed away at the age of seventy-five after an unspecified illness lasting several years. Thomas had been active in the community throughout his lifetime, particularly in the Masonic lodge where he achieved the rank of 32nd degree Mason. He was also an active member of the Odd Fellows and The Grand Army of The Republic, or GAR, a community of Civil War veterans who looked after each other. All his commitments stressed community and charity. His obituary referred to him as a pioneer resident of Spencer and one of its best citizens. By 1915 Joy was ably following his father's example of community and charitable giving, becoming one of the most beloved citizens in Spencer in his own right. He had shown that commitment quietly in 1913 and 1914 and began to garner attention in the press in 1915. He continued much the same in 1916 but by then the press was much more open to sharing the name of Spencer's new benefactor.

That year the newspapers were quick to name Joy as the person to inform if a child was in need. Starting just after Thanksgiving, the Spencer Reporter included a church note from Grace Methodist Church informing anyone who knew a child who would not be receiving a Christmas gift that they should send the names and ages to Joy Roberts. As they had the year prior, the Reporter also encouraged kids to write letters to Santa telling him what they would like to find under the tree and encouraging adults to provide information on families in need and donate cash to the cause if they were able. All donations would be given directly to Joy, who ensured the funds were well invested. The community recognized a good cause, and the newspapers encouraged everyone to do their part.

As in 1915, the Spencer Commercial Club planned the community's Christmas activities, including the festivities around the municipal Christmas Tree and they were enthusiastic about repeating the prior year's successes. The club suggested forming an organization led by local churches to monitor and facilitate charitable giving around the holidays. Most of the city's churches were represented along with members of the Women's Club and the PEO (Philanthropic Educational Organization) Society. The churches formed the Associated Charities and chose Joy to be president of the organization. Their stated mission was to have the various charities coordinate activities to ensure there was no duplication or manipulation of services.

With his credentials growing and the trust of the city behind him, Joy now had a network to aid him in increasing his reach. More children could now benefit from his generosity, and the churches had an able organizer to help them increase theirs. The following year, the newspapers moved beyond simply asking for donations and became a willful hype machine to tell Joy's story and enhance his reputation. No longer just a nice man who helped people at Christmas, he was about to get his first "promotion" to Santa's deputy from the big man himself. From his own kindness, and with the help of an ever more willing press, Joy would start making the move from able assistant, to maybe...just maybe, being Santa himself as the child in the store from chapter one would readily attest.

Three

Mr. Good Fellow

The years of 1917 through 1919 were formative years for the city of Spencer, full of pain and promise. On April 6, 1917, the United States entered World War I and many young men from Clay County were sent overseas to fight for their country. The following year marked the beginning of the Great Influenza which would claim over 600,000 lives in the United States alone. It was also a time of hope as Spencer began building a new fairground and planning to put themselves on the map with "the world's greatest county fair." Spencer wished to establish itself as the commercial and cultural center of Northwest Iowa and the fair would be the main attraction to draw tourists in. Joy Roberts would embrace the fair wholeheartedly, eventually being almost as well known for his fair activities as for his Christmas exploits.

Spencer's drive for relevance started early in its existence, before any buildings were in place. First established in 1851, Clay County initially did not even have a local government. All business related to the county ran out of Sergeant's Bluff one hundred miles away. The county was named after Henry Clay Jr., the son of former Secretary of State and three-time presidential candidate

Henry Clay. Clay Jr. had been killed in action at the Battle of Buena Vista in 1847 during the Mexican American War. In 1859, a committee formed to find an appropriate county seat and recommended Spencer based on its central location, but there was a problem. No one lived there. Speculators had already laid out a plan and cleared the area, but most residents in Clay County at the time lived in Peterson Township. When put to vote, Peterson was selected as the county seat. The area that would eventually become Spencer remained empty. Locals referred to the empty lots as Spencer Grove.

When settlers began to arrive in Spencer Grove around 1865, the new residents would have been familiar to Thomas Roberts and were likely a deciding factor in his own decision to move there. Many of the settlers were Union veterans from Wisconsin taking advantage of the Homestead Act of 1862 to make their claims, just as Thomas would five years later. In 1866, Spencer Grove Township was organized and the first schoolhouse in the area was established. The US Postal Service authorized a post office on the site in 1868, but the name Spencer Grove already existed elsewhere in Iowa, so residents dropped "Grove" and settled on Spencer as the city name.

Senator George
E. Spencer
Library of Congress

The city is named after Senator George E. Spencer, who served as a Republican senator in Alabama from 1868 to 1879. A senator from Alabama would seem to be an odd namesake for a town settled by former Union soldiers, but he was a Republican and served in Congress after the war. Born in New York, he studied law at some point in Iowa. He enlisted in the Union Army as a captain in 1862 and received a promotion to colonel when he volunteered to lead the 1st Alabama Calvary Regiment. His regiment consisted of Southern Unionists who volunteered to join the Union army, so his credentials with the Union settlers from Wisconsin were solid.

Spencer was officially founded in 1871, the year after Thomas Roberts made his soldier's claim, and later that same year replaced Peterson as the county seat. There were no buildings in town that could function as a courthouse, so the residents pooled their resources and built their own. The new structure was then purchased by the county to be used as the official county courthouse. Over the next couple of decades, railroads and telegraphs were built and Spencer's importance as a trading center increased. Clay County was primarily a farming community, so Spencer's connections to the rest of the country and ability to move crops helped it thrive. Spencer also touted itself as the place county residents could come to do their shopping, and returning to 1917, sought to become the county's entertainment center as well.

1917 saw the entrance of the United States into the war that had been raging in Europe for nearly three years. The local newspapers were full of stories about the war and ways to support the boys overseas. Spencer continued to look to a brighter future despite the dreary news, and that year the first Clay County Fair Association was established and anticipated opening the first fair during the fall of 1918, war or no war. Construction of a racetrack began and plans for the entrance were prepared. The goal was nothing short of the biggest and best county fair in all of Iowa. First, however, Spencer faced the dilemma of how to respectfully celebrate Christmas in the shadow of war. The city rallied to care for the soldiers with Joy ever ready to do his part. If letters printed during the first part of November in the Spencer News-Herald were any indication, Santa Claus himself wanted the effort to support needy children and soldiers to start early that year.

The News-Herald published two telegrams that had been sent to Spencer directly from the North Pole and Santa, the first one dated November 1 and addressed specifically to Joy Roberts. First off, Santa wanted to put to rest any question anyone might have regarding Joy's name. "Every Christmas I think of how appropriate your name is. If I had a boy I would name him 'Joy' too, for it is a name that any lad ought to be glad to have." Next, Santa asked Joy to act as his deputy with very specific duties; "to make the little boys and girls in Clay County happy again this Christmas." Lamenting that the war had nearly put him out of business, he told Joy he needed aid collecting donations to help him accomplish his tasks. Children should be encouraged to keep writing their letters as always. He also wanted to be sure the soldier boys were remembered and promised a follow up letter soon.

The next telegram arrived the following week, addressed to the editor of the News Herald. Santa again expressed his confidence in Joy's ability to complete the assignment he had been given the week before but also wanted to be sure the people of Spencer remembered to send gifts to the soldiers overseas. He had seen an advertisement the week before with the heading, "Make Christmas Merrie for the Soldier Boys," and wanted to encourage locals to be sure the businesses represented in the ad were "swamped" with orders of items to send. The rest of the message gave specific directions and dates to make sure all packages arrived before the holidays. He concluded with, "Let's all get together and make this Christmas, which in many respects will be a sad one at best, as merry as possible for the soldier boys and the kiddies, regardless of what we do for the rest of the folks."

Joy loved children but also had a heart for the soldiers. He was young enough to know several of the local boys sent to war, and as the president of the Associated Charities, he took an active role in various war efforts. He received a letter in May of 1918 from the Military Entertainment Council thanking him and his committee for organizing the sale of Smileage tickets and offering to send more advertising to assist him in his efforts. Smileage was a program that allowed people to purchase tickets for soldiers so they could attend movies and other entertainment at their military base theaters. Joy had a taste for theater and performance, so it is easy to see where the program would appeal to him. He may have also felt that he might be using Smileage tickets himself if the war continued. In an article later that holiday season, he expressed concern that it could be the last year of his work. "Next year,' he said, "will no doubt find me in the army of Uncle Sam."

The Spencer Reporter also got into the act that year, playing up Santa Claus' communications as he put Joy to work. On November 14 they reported that Santa had visited Spencer in person the day before, but quietly and behind the scenes, as it was primarily a business trip. Joy's titles began stacking up, and we again see the term "good fellows" that would be bestowed on those who donated to his cause for several years. Santa commissioned Joy as "Chief Good Fellow" for Clay County and the Reporter referred to him as Santa's first general distributor. Joy was tasked with collecting reports on all needy children and making sure no one was overlooked at Christmas. He would lead the organization of Spencer Good-fellows, where the only requirement for membership was assisting with the noble cause. As for the letters to Santa Claus written by children in the area, they could now be addressed to Santa, in care of Joy Roberts right there in Spencer, as he and Santa were "working hand in hand this Christmas."

Over the next several weeks, Joy would receive letters and deliver them to the Spencer Reporter, earning him another title; Santa's private secretary. The Reporter printed the letters from local children, telling what they wanted for Christmas. Good Fellows were encouraged to give as donations were coming in slowly that year, and for the first time we see a reference to Joy using his own money to make up shortfalls. He would rarely admit those shortages, but readers were encouraged to find Joy and say, "Joy, you've been spending your own coin making Christmas day glad for some of those kiddies who otherwise wouldn't have fared so well. I'm kicking in my little bit. Here it is." Those exact words were not necessary, of course, but the donations were appreciated whether they arrived by mail or in person.

In mid-December the News-Herald came up with a list entitled, "The Things To Do This Christmas," encouraging positive actions to counter the dreary news from the front. Citizens were encouraged to make sacrifices for the greater good, such as remembering to observe meatless, wheatless and sweetless days. Christmas fell on a meatless day, but in the spirit of the holidays, an edict from Herbert Hoover, who served as the director of the US Food Administration at the time, permitted the consumption of turkey, duck, chicken or beans that day. Other reminders related to the war effort were to donate to and join the Red Cross, send at least one package to a soldier, support the YMCA and YWCA, and write a letter to a soldier. On the home front readers were encouraged to smile, remember the children and shop early.

The list included a somewhat awkward sounding reminder to pay your debts and remember the writer because "editors eat." Despite the seemingly self-serving sentiment, to his credit, the writer saved a spot specifically for Joy with number eleven on the list. "Remember Joy Roberts. See that he gets something. He is the official Santa Claus for Spencer, when Santa himself can't be here, and he has his headquarters at the G&K Store. Go to him today and leave something for what one man has said is 'the most worthy cause of all.'"

As Christmas got closer, requests for donations slowed but the donations were always accepted. An estimated 132 children in Spencer and Clay County would enjoy a Merry Christmas who might otherwise have none without Joy and the Associated Charities. Toys would always be an exciting part of any charitable giving, but family needs had to be met as well. Joy collected or purchased clothing and shoes for children and coal for the parents so they could heat their homes. The Spencer Reporter, like the News-Herald, made an appeal specifically for Joy. They pointed out that Joy spent his own time and money without asking for help, but he would still gratefully accept any donations given. "Joy didn't tell the writer this. He doesn't even know it is going to appear this week in your Reporter. But Joy isn't a man with millions and he hadn't ought to have to spend his own time and his own money, too." Joy did not always bring in as much as he put toward his work, but he would ensure that every child had a happy Christmas regardless.

When Christmas arrived, the Reporter declared the festivities a "red letter day in Spencer." The city streets were lined with thirty Christmas trees, and 1,019 children joined the parade that year. The crowds overwhelmed local stores with last-minute shopping and Santa Claus made his promised appearance along with Mrs. Claus. The celebrity couple arrived in a large truck and were greeted by Joy and Miss Elizabeth Steigleder as Joy continued his role as Santa's able assistant. Joy and Miss Steigleder escorted them throughout their visit, and local Boy Scouts provided an honor guard. The festivities were a success, charitable giving praiseworthy, and despite the ongoing war, a very merry time was had by all in Spencer.

Spencer, Tuesday, Wednesday, Thursday, Friday of Next Week—September **24, 25, 26, 27**

Four big day and two monster night programs at one of the finest fair and exposition grounds in Iowa

View of Clay County Fair Grounds as it will look when completed.   The principal buildings and many of the improvements are already built

Advertisement for the first Clay County Fair

Spencer Reporter

1918 began with eager anticipation in Spencer as the city continued to prepare for the first ever Clay County Fair. The fair would start on September 24 and run through September 27. When the fair arrived, it opened to great fanfare. The first day included a patriotic parade to show support for the continuing war. Soldiers were present to serve as security and Governor William L. Harding gave a speech to dedicate the new fairgrounds. Longtime Spencer resident and community leader Bob Keir was thirteen years old during the first fair and like most young boys seemed to enjoy getting dirty. His memories of the fair included the greased pole contest and the greased pig. "That pig was slippery," he recalled so he must have taken a shot at it himself.

Bob Keir lived to the remarkable age of 106 years old. He remembered Joy in a variety of settings beyond the fair and Christmas. Joy had a love for holidays in general, and Bob remembered looking out his window as a boy and seeing Joy on Saint Patrick's Day "decked out in green from head to foot." Many years later others would recall that Joy always enjoyed a good Halloween prank. His friends would often refer to him as "Joker." There is no mention of Joy specifically during the first year of the fair, but he was involved from the beginning. He had many duties over the years, but when asked what he did, he would often retort that he was the "supervisor of wild women."

When the fair ended, the local newspapers declared it a great success and claimed that officials from other county fairs across Iowa "could hardly believe their eyes, so great was the fair." A total of 33,000 attended the fair and the receipts added up to almost $16,000, the best in the state. The Clay County Fair Association could not have been more pleased with the results and were already looking for ways to make the next fair bigger and better. Within a couple of years, locals were referring to it as the world's greatest county fair, and by 1928 that became the official slogan for the fair and is still in use today. Spencer entered the month of October with every right to be proud and in high spirits going into the holiday season, and when the war ended on November 11, it seemed Christmas would be one of the brightest in memory. A shadow was building though, as the world moved from one tragedy to another when the Great Influenza took nearly as many lives worldwide in four months as the war had taken in four years.

During the last year of the war, countries were aware of the flu but hesitant to report on it with the war still ongoing and bringing in enough bad news. Spain did not participate in the war, so the press there reported on the spreading threat more than in other countries. The outbreak became known as the Spanish flu due to the mistaken impression that it began there. In the United States, the first strain of the flu appeared in the Midwest in March of 1918

A temporary hospital set up in the gymnasium at Iowa State University
Iowa State University Photographs

but seemed relatively mild. When the second strain hit in August, no one was prepared for the high mortality rates to come. The second strain put so much pressure on the immune system that the healthier one's immune system, the harder they were hit as their bodies overcompensated. Adults between the ages of twenty and forty years old were the hardest hit, and as a result the disease spread quickly in military camps as soldiers moved from base to base.

In Iowa, the flu hit Fort Dodge. In a twelve-hour period on October 8, 996 new cases were diagnosed and before it was over, there were 10,000 cases on that base alone resulting in over 700 deaths. In the last three months of 1918, the Iowa State Board of Health reported 6,116 deaths in the state from the flu with another 3,085 dying of pneumonia, a common condition among people weakened by the flu who might have survived otherwise. In addition to reports of the lives taken by illness, the papers were also full of sad news from the war. News traveled slowly and while families were happy the war had ended, there was still uncertainty about their loved ones overseas. There were many stories between November 11 and the end of the year telling of families who found out late that their sons were lost in the final month of the war.

The result was an unusual mix in the newspapers of trying to boost holiday spirits while readers were constantly reminded of the suffering around them. Seeking to offer some levity during hard times, once again, a letter appeared from Santa Claus in the Spencer Reporter addressed to Joy. Santa let Joy know he had been busy all year making thousands of toys and goodies for the children and was excited about returning to Spencer again. He asked Joy to be his advance agent and special representative. He wanted children to write to him and for adults to give generously to Joy's work. Letters could be sent to Joy as he would be sure to forward them to Santa, and Santa once again planned to attend the municipal Christmas celebration.

1918 was the year the term Good Fellows became official. During a meeting of the Spencer Commercial Club, members expressed their appreciation of Joy's efforts over the previous five years. Many understood that while Joy had received donations, he always had to use his own money in the end to cover the costs. Club president, O.A. Bjornstad recommended that members give Joy $50 to kick off his campaign, but the idea met with resistance. Rather than donating money as a club, the members wanted to give individually and voted to form an official Good Fellows Club in Spencer using the two local newspapers as a means of communicating the needs of the club. The papers would print the names of those who donated in recognition of their generosity. At the end of the night the members raised $32 to start things off.

After a few years running the Associated Charities, no one doubted Joy's ability to care for the needy. Both the Spencer Reporter and the Spencer News-Herald enthusiastically touted the Good Fellows Club and unselfishly acknowledged the other's role, committing to working together. The News-Herald exclaimed that Joy was the "main squeeze" at the meeting and gave him high praise for his efforts. "No other man in the entire country is so well versed in that sort of work as he and no other would have available the means of telling the needy from the unworthy as it is said that Joy has on file the name, age, and condition of every child in the county." Just like Santa Claus, Joy appeared to have a list of who had been naughty and who had been nice.

The Reporter also made a direct plea to their readers, asking, "If you don't read another line of this 28-page issue, the editors want you to read this one clear through." They hoped to raise enough funds to ensure that at the end of the holiday season, Joy would not have to use his own money. Anticipating there would be money left over, readers were assured that any funds remaining would be deposited into a fund to draw interest to be used the following year or turned over to the Associated Charities for use during the year as needs arose outside of the holidays. Joy was officially dubbed Mr. Good Fellow and had the official backing of the leading businessmen in town and the press. Their goal was to raise at least $100 that holiday season.

The following week, the Reporter laid it on thick to push people to give to needy children. "You must have a withered up heart, indeed, if you cannot be reached by this plea." They argued that all little children want to have a merry Christmas and are not old enough to understand when Santa skips over them. "They don't know the conditions," possibly referring to the lingering effects of the flu and hardships of poverty in general. Organizations were encouraged to make five-dollar donations, and individuals could give as little as a dime, so long as everyone in the community was willing to give something. Emphasis focused on the spirit of giving, not the amount.

When Christmas rolled around, both newspapers announced that Mr. Good Fellow was ready to go. Joy anticipated being up all night on Christmas Eve preparing to make his deliveries Christmas Day. He had a list of over 150 children, and each child would have a gift appropriate for their age and labeled with their name to avoid any errors. Not only kids, however, as it was noted that some "extremely old people" would also be receiving gifts if there was concern about them being neglected on the holidays. Joy happily reported that he had enough for every home in danger of being missed by Santa Claus.

Joy never took much of a break even when the holidays ended. He looked forward to the next Christmas and through the Associated Charities helped others throughout the year as needs arose. He always found time for the Clay County Fair though, and in 1919 his reputation for selling tickets began to rise. In a book about the history of Spencer published forty-five years later entitled "*Here is Yesterday*," Don Buchan noted three highlights of the 1919 fair. A wrestling match between local boys Ralph Parcaut and Jud Thompson that garnered a great deal of interest. Rube Liebman made his first appearance. He was an entertainer and announcer who went by "Hiram" on stage. The third highlight deemed worthy of mention praised Joy Roberts for selling $500 of advanced tickets by himself.

The fair started on September 23 with one change requested. Attendees were asked not to smoke in the barns. On the day before the fair began, disaster nearly struck when someone flicked cigarette ashes into hay in one of the display barns leading to the ban. The fair was once again a financial success. The main concern following the fair focused on the need for more buildings due to the size of the exhibits and the enthusiasm of exhibitors and concessionaires to get in on the ever-growing spectacle. Joy eagerly took up the challenge of helping the fair grow, working behind the scenes, always ready to make a sale. The following year, the Spencer-Herald warned people to have their money ready, because once Joy got a hold of them, they would not be able to get away without spending a few dollars on season tickets.

The newspaper coverage of Joy's Christmas activities in 1919 was light compared to the previous two years. The first article in early December did not report on Joy's usual Christmas giving but rather focused on the need to raise money for the Associated Charities to rent space in town. A room was needed that would give them somewhere to repair and distribute clothes for the needy. Winters can be harsh in Spencer and the need for clothing would always rise as colder weather arrived. Two weeks after the first request, Joy announced that a room had been provided in the basement of the Spencer News-Herald office. He continued with his own annual Christmas giving, but without the playfulness the newspapers had added in previous years.

The Good Fellows raised over $400 for the Christmas fund that year. Santa Claus was expected in town again and planning to cruise up and down Main Street handing out candy to children. Commercial Club activities took precedence in the press over Joy's annual Christmas trip to visit the needy, but he did get credit for his efforts with the Associated Charities, giving out warm clothing to those who could use it. The Commercial Club considered the idea of having Santa Claus fly over Spencer in an "aeroplane," but maybe with Joy's frugalness in mind, decided the cost would take money away from the true goal of giving. The money saved would be turned over to Joy and the Associated Charities for more clothing.

As the new decade arrived, an article appeared around fair time in 1920 illustrating that Joy's giving and civic involvements were year-round commitments and not just a Christmas whim. The article detailed his ticket sales for the fair again but also highlighted other activities. Joy was the county chairman for the Salvation Army and used that job to "keep young lads on the right path." He also oversaw the programs at a three-day Round Up, a western show and rodeo, in July. He did such a good job that the promoter, R.C. Bangs, asked Joy to go to Rochester, Minnesota with him to assist with the next show. If an opportunity presented itself to advertise and promote life in Spencer, Joy would fully commit to it.

Santa Remembering the Poor in Spencer Last Year

Spencer News-Herald

While articles were not as prominent around Christmas in 1919, in 1920 a picture was printed from the previous year showing Santa Claus, possibly Joy himself in the red suit, in front of a horse-drawn sleigh. The heading said, "Santa Remembering the Poor in Spencer Last Year." The image was reprinted often over the next couple of years to remind people of his generosity. The 1920s brought in an age of hope and prosperity as America recovered from the hard times of war and disease, and with a few exceptions early in the decade, Joy enjoyed a time of reciprocal generosity from the community and his legion of Good Fellows.

Four

Every Child Must Be Happy

The Spencer Commercial Club organized the 1920 Christmas activities in Spencer with Joy offering his usual assistance while continuing his own charitable giving. When asked to report on the municipal Christmas tree expenses from the prior year, Joy deferred, saying he did not recall how much the tree cost, but he did remember that 176 children were given candy and presents. J.H. McCord, a club member, quickly jumped in to support Joy with a heartfelt plea. "The Christmas spirit exhibited in Spencer the last few years has been a beautiful thing. If Joy Roberts were not in the room, I would say that he is one of the blessings of this town. Mr. Roberts ought not to have to spend any of his own money. To think—175 kids made happy. Is it too much to ask that we do it again? Let's give these 175 babies another happy Christmas."

His appeal proved inspirational. J.L. Brunais moved that the club set up a subscription to cover the costs associated with the municipal tree and offered five dollars to start the fund. Others followed, and in just ten minutes club members raised $260. Earl Moore offered to donate a tree and Ben Shine offered to transport it to Main Street. Joy took charge of the distribution of gifts again. He would collect and repair old toys, a practice from his first Christmas as Santa in 1913 that would become his primary calling in years to come. Club members were concerned because Joy had donated forty dolls and fifty toys at his own expense the year prior and they hoped to help him defray some of the costs for the upcoming holiday. Joy never seemed to give it as much thought as those around him. He appreciated any assistance but would always move forward with or without it.

The Spencer Reporter once again referred to Joy as Santa's chief assistant, but the News-Herald upgraded him after the meeting. Joy, as far as they were concerned, had been Spencer's official Santa for six years. That title would stick for most of his life and long after his passing. Joy did not mind being Santa's assistant, however, and worked hard to plan another celebration. Children could collect tickets in advance to hand to Santa during the Christmas Eve parade in exchange for bags of candy that had been prepared by the Professional Women's League and local Sunday school classes. Santa upgraded his transportation to an automobile, an easier and more modern way to get around than his usual sleigh. When the big day arrived, Santa handed out 1,083 bags of candy to local children. An additional thirty-two families were given Christmas baskets full of gifts and food items allowing them to prepare a traditional Christmas dinner.

Joy's family kept clippings from local newspapers, many of which are still safely tucked away and in good condition. An undated article from the News-Herald, presumably from this early 1920's timeframe, described his usual Christmas Day routine in detail. He worked "night and day" for three days prior to Christmas preparing baskets and wrapping gifts. He spent hours on Christmas Day driving around the county "dressed as the good old man,

gay in his bell adorned red costume." He waved at children gawking out their windows as he passed and brought gifts to 164 children that year. Joy always made sure to thank the children, his
friends, and all the local merchants who made his giving possible.

Joy started preparing for next Christmas as soon as the current
one ended but never failed to take a summer break for the Clay
County Fair. Prior to the 1921 fair, the News-Herald predicted Joy
would sell more tickets alone than the rest of the committee in
charge of sales put together. In 1919 he sold $500 worth of tick-
ets, and over $1,400 the next year, more than half of the total sea-
son tickets presales, so the prediction had precedent. Readers were
again warned to have their $1.90 ready if they saw Joy coming. He
was touted as the "man behind" at the fair. He had no set position
but thrived as the "official season ticket seller, advertiser, booster
and all-around handyman for the fair." The fair saw record crowds
as it continued to grow.

The 1920s were a time when more people were able to give, but
times were not good for all. The News-Herald lamented that many
people were going through hard times financially. In 1921 the newspapers put out the usual appeals for Christmas giving, with heavy
emphasis on the need for warm clothing. Joy called for donations
of clothing in early December. At a Commercial Club meeting Joy
did not attend, members were told he was already $100 behind and
using his own money to compensate. The members voted to set
up tripods and kettles that are so familiar nowadays to encourage
more giving from the public, and they raised $30 during the short
time they were available.

Christmas planning went on as usual, but Joy shared his concerns that there were still two months of winter after Christmas.
Reports of families without proper clothing or shoes, with no beds
and no covers, and no coal to heat their homes dominated the

headlines more than Christmas needs. Joy once again procured an empty room in town to collect donated clothing. The needs that year were great, but people were willing to help. The newspapers asked any person or organization planning to visit families at Christmas or thereafter to contact Joy, who would coordinate the visits to ensure no duplication of effort, and no home would be missed.

The Christmas festivities were a success "in spite of the extreme cold." Final tallies showed that forty-two families were visited and given baskets containing food, supplies, and of course toys. 132 children from those families were provided with gifts and goodies. At the municipal celebration, 1,200 sacks of candy were given to children present and in a rare admission, the News-Herald confirmed that Joy played the part of Santa Claus. Many children were beginning to assume he was the real Santa anyway, so the newspapers had no fear of ruining their belief. Joy would continue to give out clothing from his donated room, but many people were beginning to feel Santa had earned an upgrade.

The winter of 1923 started off looking like it might be considerably milder compared to the previous year, but that could change, so Joy started early with requests for clothing. He did not need to rent a room, however. Santa would have his own cottage built for collecting donations, handing out candy and gifts, and storing old clothing when the holidays were over. The community planned to build a northern style cottage, complete with snow on the roof, evergreen trees and a fireplace. All materials necessary would be donated by local sources and the cottage would even have electric lighting and a telephone. The Commercial Club planned to use the 8 x 12-foot structure to hold a vote in mid-December, but that mattered little to children were thrilled with the city's new holiday attraction. On December 23 it would be the center of attention

Santa Claus and his "sleigh" next to the Christmas cottage

during the Christmas festivities. Kids could collect their candy at the cottage rather than brave traffic at the municipal Christmas tree which usually stood in the middle of Main Street.

Local businesses and the city donated the necessary lumber, hardware, decorations and wiring. They also provided a heating stove, telephone and electricity. The businesses included the Schoeneman Bros., J.F. Anderson, and Floete lumber companies, C. Ben Bjornstad company, Frink Bros., Fred Nelson and Hans Fries, and the Western Electric Telephone Company. Frank Deigaard, Metz Anderson, Theo Miller, Elmer Green, Jens Thompson and John Smith provide the carpentry work and labor. J.K. West painted the cottage with paint provided by the Otto A. Bjornstad company and Wilson Grain donated five hundred pounds of coal to keep it warm. It was a city-wide effort. The Commercial Club raised over $400 to add to donations of food and clothing from other businesses and individuals.

The News-Herald gave Joy a lot of press but also remembered contributions from other generous citizens. V. Blaine Asher understood that children love to give as well as receive, so he offered "brand new shiny quarters" to children so they could do their own shopping. He gave out 190 quarters totaling $47.50 from his own pocket. Walter H. Thomas gave Joy a check for $25 and said he would give more if needed to make every child happy. That fit well with Joy's motto, which was "EVERY child must be happy on Christmas Day." He did not recognize social boundaries and made sure gifts were given "without publicity or show of benevolence." The newspapers were his means of collecting donations, but he did not seek attention for attention's sake.

Quqrters for Christmas

Y. BLAINE ASHER

The Offcial 'Santa'

E. JOY ROBERTS

Another article the same day, also in the News-Herald, stated unequivocally that Joy had helped more people in Spencer than any other. Looking back on the previous decade, the article recalled how for the first few years Joy did his work alone but became so successful that the Commercial Club took notice and offered to help him financially. When Christmas came around, the successful pairing saw to it that 1,400 children received bags of candy at the new cottage, and forty-two families received a visit from Spencer's Santa. Blaine Asher handed out quarters from the Motor Supply building on Main Street. Between the candy and quarters, children enjoyed a splendid holiday, and between the giving and efforts to build the new cottage, the entire community could take pride in their contributions to the generous holiday spirit.

In the weeks following Christmas, Joy stayed in the news and public eye thanks to another one of his occasional pursuits. Spencer put on frequent home talent shows giving residents the opportunity to show their skills in various types of entertainment. On New Year's Day at the Spencer Opera House, traveling home talent show director Rosella Zura put on a musical comedy play entitled "The Masquerade Party" that she had written herself. Joy played one of the lead characters, Father Weber. The proceeds for the show were donated to the Sons of Veterans, a group dedicated to preserving the history of former Union soldiers. Being the son of a Civil War veteran himself, it is easy to see where Joy would be excited to give his time and talent to the cause.

Joy's talent for advertising was on display again prior to the 1923 Clay County Fair and needed due to changes forced upon fairgoers. The state attorney general ruled that games of chance were against state law despite their popularity so fair officials responded by promising more concessions. The fair made a nice profit despite the loss of those popular activities, but there were concerns about a lower number of season ticket sales in advance. Joy did his part, selling 350 of 1,000 season tickets, implementing a creative way to draw attention to himself. A week before the fair started, he wired his car for electricity and covered it with lights, then parked on Main Street to conduct his sales. This was tame compared to some of the elaborate creations he would come up with in the future, but for now at least he found use for his Christmas lights outside of the holiday season.

Joy would put those lights to good use again come Christmastime. The first big holiday announcement proclaimed the return of Santa's cottage. It would serve the same purposes as the previous year and, of course, be brightly lit and decorated. The Commercial Club donated $400 during their first holiday meeting to assist Joy, breaking their previous record. A report from that meeting made a curious claim, saying Joy had tried to step down from his duties on occasion, but no one would agree to replace him and neither the city nor Joy himself would allow him to quit if it meant children might be left behind. Joy stayed on the job. That Christmas was one of the warmest Christmases in recent memory with above freezing temperatures and no snow, making deliveries easy. Joy introduced Forest Roberts in the Santa suit, and his volunteers, labeled the "Santa Claus corps" by the press, visited forty-one families and 143 children.

As Joy's reputation and popularity grew, his "corps" may have suggested taking a bigger step in his efforts for the residents of Spencer. In March of 1924, he threw his hat into a new arena, the political arena, announcing a run for mayor. There were four candidates. Eugene Bender was a former mayor and W.E. Long a former city council member. Joy and T.J. O'Donnell were the outsiders of the group, but many supporters thought they had the qualifications to do a good job despite never having held a public office. Both could expect a decent number of votes, and this created some tension during the election season. There were some who felt adding two additional candidates could hurt the field as they drew votes from the two more serious candidates.

Joy's camp seemed to understand the concerns, stating that his reputation "as Santa Claus and friend of the needy" ensured he would sway some voters away from both Long and Bender. In the end, experience won the day. Long was elected mayor with 1,015 votes followed by Bender with 922. Joy came in distant third with 113 votes to O'Donnell's seventy. Grateful for the votes, Joy promised future efforts in his post-election statement. "I want to thank each and every one for your vote and the kind things that you have said whether you voted for me or not and will try to have a majority next time as great as I had altogether this time."

That summer Joy participated in another community event, and on a grand scale. On August 7 and 8, Clay County held a big historical pageant to celebrate the county's past and present. The event boasted a cast of nearly 1,000 Clay County residents. It was performed outdoors at the fairgrounds with proceeds going to the Clay County Fair Association and the American Legion. Joy joined many in the crowded cast acting as the earliest settlers of Clay County. His 13-year-old daughter Joyce participated in the "Dance of the Dawn" alongside a slightly younger Grace Roberts. They were part of a larger group dressed up to represent the sunrise. Grace Roberts, along with Forest Roberts who played Santa Claus at Christmas may have been related to Joy and his family, but the relationship is not clear.

Joy headed back to the fairgrounds the following month, of course. It promised to be a big year for the Clay County Fair, and "big" was the key word thrown around often in the advertising and buildup. For the first time, the fair would expand, running five days instead of the usual four. The attraction continued to grow and was a financial success. Organizers were quick to point out that the first four days would have beat the previous fairs in terms of revenue and attendance even without the extra day. The fifth day simply added to the success. The spotlight afterwards rightly focused on the overall success and not on how many tickets Joy sold in advance, and he likely reveled in that success and in the extra day to promote his favorite event.

When Christmas came in 1924, the warm Christmas of the prior year seemed a distant memory as another harsh winter took hold. Joy once again took charge of both the Christmas activities and cold weather relief. He felt needs would be greater than in previous years, whether from the cold or from a downturn in employment, and shared his concerns with the local newspaper. "There are more men out of work than usual and there will be plenty of need for relief work all through the winter. The winter will be cold and disagreeable, and coal and food have to be bought as well as clothing, and in addition, we want to see to it that the kiddies are remembered with toys and candy and nuts and all those things."

The local community made sure to give Joy kudos for his efforts as they always had. The Spencer Reporter said Spencer should be congratulated for having a citizen like Joy who willingly took on relief work without asking anything in return. The Commercial Club gave him a vote of confidence and offered their ringing endorsement. "That we endorse the Joy Roberts activities and give him our full confidence and endorsement for his work and ask that the president of the Commercial Club name a committee to raise additional funds to be placed at Mr. Roberts' disposal for his Christmas activities and relief work." Joy felt he needed at least $1,000, and both the Commercial Club and local newspapers were once again fully on board to assist him with raising those funds.

The Santa Claus cottage had officially been repurposed. It now sat in Joy's yard and served as storage for donated clothing and larger gifts. Santa's official headquarters would be in a room next to Citizen's National Bank. The bank donated the room to Joy, and he quickly went to work setting up his holiday decorations. He set up a display in a window facing the street and added a Christmas tree and imitation fireplace on the inside. He filled a small area in back with toys and books, and all the snack bags that were going to be handed out that year. Cards were given to children entitling them to one snack bag each. Santa arrived at his new headquarters on December 23, and aided by Joy, passed out bags to nearly five hundred children.

On Christmas Eve, Joy made his annual rounds delivering gifts, visiting forty-six families and 145 children. He was aided in his efforts by E.L. Goyette, who had also helped Joy the previous two years. Mr. Goyette would offer the use of his dray to carry packages to their final destinations. A dray is a horse drawn cart. Joy often partnered with friends who were willing to provide transportation for his holiday giving. He enjoyed decorating whatever mode of transportation he used and making them memorable. Two years earlier, he had used Christmas lights to light up his car while selling fair tickets. For the 1925 Clay County Fair, he was even more creative.

The Spencer News-Herald credited Joy as being "the handiest man at the Clay County Fair." They claimed that over the previous seven years he had driven thousands of miles to promote the fair. A long list of duties included "taking up fence placards, distributing advertising cards, selling season tickets, helping classify and locate entries and doing a thousand and one other things that only Joy knows how to do." During the build up to the 1925 fair Joy shared some of his driving duties with Jimmy Sloan, who coordinated racing activities that year and who designed and built a realistic replica of a railroad engine to advertise the auto races and the Clay County Fair in general. It seems likely that Joy would park the engine at his usual location on Main Street to sell season tickets, and he and Mr. Sloan used it to travel to other communities the rest of the time.

Mr. Sloan and Joy painted the engine black and yellow and built it over a Ford chassis. The exhaust was designed to exit through a smokestack to give the appearance of a real railroad engine as it traveled through town. It included a whistle and a

Something Unique in the Way of Advertising

Replica steam engine built to advertise for the fair
Spencer News-Herald

bell, and by all accounts looked like an actual train in motion. Joy would usually make a circuit around Northwest Iowa for his advertising. Jimmy Sloan took his railroad engine to the Palo Alto County Fair that year, which was local, but also drove to Clarinda and as far away as Davenport, over three hundred miles away. The engine, which the News-Herald called "something new in the way of advertising," received well-deserved attention at each location it visited, and brought a lot of positive publicity for the Clay County Fair and its ever-growing footprint.

For Christmas in 1925, Joy had several new ideas as well. The season started with the usual Commercial Club meetings and endorsements. The club gave him $400 from their charity budget and put him in charge of all charitable giving again. He made a point to emphasize all giving should be voluntary. R.W. Hanson offered the use of a room in front of his building as headquarters and for the first new idea to advertise Joy's activities, D.H. Wollam and the M.& W. Poster Company offered a free illustrated poster. The poster lit up every evening for maximum exposure. It read, "Be a Good Fellow; subscribe to the Joy Roberts Christmas Fund. We want Santa to visit EVERY kid in Spencer this year."

Another new idea changed how and where children would receive their bags of candy. Joy prepared 1,500 bags but instead of parading the children down cold streets to the Christmas tree or cottage, they were congregated together in a warm movie theater. H.N. Davies offered a free movie showing for Christmas that year. The local newspapers were weeklies, however, so the last-minute offer did not get out to the public via usual advertising methods. Joy, hearing of the offer, used his large and effective network to get the exiting word around town quickly. Nine hundred children piled into the theater and received the same treatment as regular paying customers, with organ music, newsreels and the showing of a comedy called "The Broncho Express." All nine hundred children received bags of candy, with the remaining bags saved for future use.

Joy oversaw the party inside the theater. The News-Herard called Joy "the man who has made more hearts throb with pleasure and more eyes shine with delight than any other man in town no doubt." He continued to spread that happiness a few days later when he made his annual rounds, handing out not only toys, but clothing, groceries and coal, to eighty-six families and 184 children. As usual, Joy did not slow down after Christmas. There were still two cold months of winter remaining and money to be raised for the cause, so Joy came up with another unique idea to get things done. He was going to direct his own home talent show with all proceeds going to the Good Fellows organization.

The play, entitled "The Early Bird," consisted of three acts, with vaudeville performances and other entertainment planned between the acts. Joy was the do-it-all behind the show, directing, advertising, casting, and playing the lead role of Mr. Barnaby Bird, an elderly gentleman who enjoyed a bit too much champagne throughout the play. Earl Tangney and Ed Robinson assisted Joy with the directing, and the entire cast consisted of residents from around the area. Planned for two nights, the show ended up playing for three, and when all expenses were accounted for, the show earned a profit of $174 for Joy's charity. The reviews from the audience were complimentary and Joy was again the toast of the city, which may have come in handy when he announced his return to a previous platform. Joy decided to run for mayor one more time.

As always Joy had support from many people who were impressed by his giving spirit and willingness to help others. Comments from potential voters were recorded by the local newspapers. "He knows the rich and poor alike and is the friend of them all." "He has the time to devote to office." "Joy is always ready to lend a helping hand; we want him for mayor." Those statements were all true. The impression that he had a lot of time to devote to the office probably derived from the amount of time he spent on his Christmas activities. He had a day job as an insurance agent, however, and did have work to do. He was also competitive by nature as his days as a college football player would indicate, so when his company started a contest for top insurance sales right before the election, politics took a back seat as he dove headlong into the competition.

Joy declared in a headline, "I Am Out To Win!" He was not talking about the race for mayor, however, but announcing his decision to drop out of the election. Joy worked for The Travelers Insurance of Hartford and the company had initiated a contest to see which agent could turn in the most applications during the last part of March. Joy wanted to win "the BIG PRIZE" and no mayoral race was going to get in his way. Even if he did not win the big prize, "I surely am going to win one of the smaller ones." He asked prospective voters to come see him and ask about his $6 accident policy. Given his propensity for selling Clay County Fair season tickets, he seemed justified in his enthusiasm. He still managed to get one vote for mayor from a supporter who seemingly would not be dissuaded. He never stated if he won the prize at work.

When the fair rolled around, the usual articles referring to Joy as the handiest man at the fair and touting his many duties appeared again. More intriguing, we get a rare mention of the woman behind the handiest man in the fair, Joy's wife Lena. Referred to in the preferred method of the day as Mrs. E. Joy Roberts, Lena oversaw an information bureau near

Spencer News-Herald

the fair gates, accessible from both sides. Her job involved collecting information from visitors and creating a list of volunteers who were willing to rent rooms in their homes for those fair visitors coming from outside the area. Her area of responsibility also included the lost and found department for the fair. Lena always fully supported Joy in his efforts, so it is nice to see that she got her share of appreciation in the local newspapers.

There were many familiar events during the 1926 Christmas season, but overall, it proved a difficult year for giving. Two free movies were offered for children. One of the movies played at the Spencer Opera House where Joy had set up his headquarters in a room on the second floor. Any donation, of money or supplies, covered the cost of admission and the show generated roughly $25 for the Good Fellows fund. Bags of candy were handed out at the second movie showing for children, this time at the Frasier theater. The nine hundred bags were funded by the Commercial Club. The poster from the year before advertising Joy's Christmas fund was upgraded to a full-size billboard on the exterior of Otto J. Bjornstad's drug store. Despite the bevy of familiar activities, however, the Good Fellows fund did not bring in the usual donations, which was unfortunate but would not dissuade Joy from meeting his holiday goals.

In late 1926, there were multiple bank failures around Northwest Iowa. Banks were either closing permanently or scrambling to stay afloat by asking their clients to agree to deposit money and not withdraw those deposits for a set amount of time, usually several months. Two banks in Spencer were saved in this manner, so it is possible that donations usually earmarked for Joy were limited by local efforts to save the banks. By December 22 Joy raised only $26 and as a result had to borrow money to cover his expenses. The News-Herald headline on December 23 lamented there would be "Many Empty Baskets at Christmas This Year." When all was said and done, Joy managed to deliver baskets to thirty-seven families and 146 children, but the costs were more than $175 over his available funds with no sure solution regarding how the losses were to be recovered.

In 1927 there were no reports about Joy borrowing money or going into debt, but there were whispers about how charitable giving should be handled going forward. Conversations within the Commercial Club speculated on whether it was appropriate for a commercial organization to also operate as a charity. A new Public Welfare Association had recently formed, and many hoped that they could take over the charitable works. All agreed on the merits of Joy's activities, and in the end the club donated $200 to Joy with the understanding that it would be used for candy, nuts and toys for children but not for other items such as food and clothing which were handled by the new welfare association. Going forward there would be less mention of the Commercial Club's role in support of Joy's holiday giving as the welfare association and other charitable organizations took the lead.

Joy's headquarters moved to the basement of the Spencer Reporter building in 1927. He encouraged children to go there and get tickets for the free movie showing at the Solon Theater where they would get their usual bags of candy. After a brief two-day weather delay, kids arrived to watch their free movie and get candy. When Christmas Eve came, Joy delivered his holiday packages to thirty-seven families and 154 children. He received top billing for the charitable efforts as "the cities official 'Santa Claus,'" but the efforts of local churches and organizations were lauded as well. The first year of the Public Welfare Association was a success.

The combination of the Commercial Club, the Public Welfare Association and Joy Roberts continued to function well as the 1928 holiday season approached. There were no movies that year, but the annual snack bag handouts were planned as usual, to be distributed in the Commercial Club rooms. Santa Claus would be the guest of honor, and Joy appointed "a committee of one" to make sure Santa received proper attention during his visit. Joy also ensured that the candy bags were ready to go on time. The welfare association took charge of the food baskets to be handed out to needy families while Joy and the Epworth League handled the toys. As usual, all efforts were coordinated to ensure no duplication of efforts.

The newspapers went back to their old habits of celebrating Joy and his role as Santa Claus to so many needy children. The News-Herald exclaimed that "He is better acquainted with the poor children of the city than any other person who resides here." He prepared 1,400 bags of candy with the help of local youth, including Joyce and Charles, now seventeen and twelve respectively. When the day came to hand out the candy, both children were still at his side. The Spencer Reporter claimed, "the satisfaction he has gotten out of his philanthropic work is all the reward he has ever received or ever asked for," but he always appreciated hearing a sincere "thank you."

On Christmas Eve, Joy distributed toys and baskets to thirty-eight families and 142 children, driving in a car donated by N.E. Driscoll. The roads were in good condition as 1928 was one of the warmest Christmases on record. The good weather also helped local merchants achieve record sales in some cases and they reported customers coming in from further outside Spencer than ever before. The sales and successful charitable giving seemed to indicate brighter times ahead for Spencer and for Joy's activities, but 1929 would bring silence in the local newspapers and considerably more work for the Public Welfare Association as hard times descended on Iowa, and on America as a whole.

Five

We Have Faith In Spencer

After 1928, Joy received considerably less press in local newspapers at Christmastime even though his charitable efforts continued. There are no newspaper records available for December 1929. The next mention of Joy around Christmas appeared in 1930 when he provided the Spencer News-Herald with old letters to Santa he had collected from 1915 to 1918. Curiously, the Herald referred to Joy as "formerly Santa's official representative in Spencer." Throughout the 1930's, the Herald promoted itself as Santa's mail collector in Spencer, and that continued through 1937 when the paper folded and merged with another local newspaper. It would be presumptive to find any malice in the decision to curtail the coverage Joy received, and it may have simply been a new way for the paper to market itself. It may also have been the result of major social upheavals at the time.

It is not clear why there are no newspaper records available from around Christmas 1929. The last edition of the News-Herald prior to Christmas printed on October 24, 1929. History knows that date better as "Black Thursday," widely accepted as the start of the Great Depression. It may be a coincidence. The records from the Spencer Reporter are also missing for Christmas and restart in the spring of 1930 around the same time as the Herald. Those records would be convenient now, but there were bigger concerns that year. The Great Depression would have a significant impact on how charities operated and gave rise to many new charitable organizations. Joy's visibility in the press probably suffered due to global needs overshadowing local needs and an inability for people to give, as happened in 1926 when local banks were in danger of failing.

The bank closures, or near closures, in 1926 were part of a larger issue impacting banks throughout the 1920s, especially in rural areas. During World War I the government gave farmers high prices for their products, so many borrowed extra from the banks to buy more land, increasing the price of farmland considerably. When the war ended, surplus production continued but the prices dropped and eventually plummeted. Farmers who had taken out loans could no longer pay the banks, the banks could not pay their depositors, and many banks closed as a result. Farmers started going bankrupt and losing their farms to foreclosures. Northwest Iowa, being primarily a farming community, was hit hard and some farmers took out their anger by lashing out at those they felt were responsible.

In nearby Le Mars, where Lena Roberts had gone to college, several farmers stormed a courtroom and removed the presiding judge. Taking him out of town, they attempted to force the judge to stop all foreclosure proceedings, but he refused. The farmers threatened to hang him, but cooler heads eventually prevailed. The National Guard was called in and arrested several of the ringleaders, but the frustration continued. After Black Thursday, the financial crisis began to hit cities as well as farms and poverty spread. Spencer became one of many towns with a shantytown, a settlement of poorly constructed homes, or shacks, with little or no sanitation or other basic services housing impoverished families. These poor communities would have been a high priority for Joy, with or without the support of the press.

In the late 1930s, when Joy's charitable giving began to make news again and his popularity in the press was restored, most sources confirm he had never stopped his Christmas efforts for the needy children of Spencer and Clay County. He regularly dressed as Santa Claus for holiday events in Spencer and carried on with his giving to the best of his ability. He by no means disappeared from the press in the 1930s, however, as he still dabbled in politics and took his commitments to the Clay County Fair to another level, especially when it came to advertising.

Joyce Roberts was the first family member to show up in the newspapers that decade when she graduated from high school in 1930. Joy appeared next with the usual summary of his fair responsibilities as aid to Secretary Leo. C. Daily a few months later. Joy's love of and involvement with the fair had been a constant topic during the 1920s, often revolving around his ability to sell season tickets to anyone. In 1930 he continued to add more responsibilities, such as the distribution of advertising in the areas around Spencer prior to the event and working on various tasks during the fair itself. He worked in a similar capacity for the Iowa State Fair and used his position there to advertise the county fair at every opportunity.

After sharing his letters to Santa Claus at Christmas, his next appearance in the press had nothing to do with charity or the fair. It was a brief mention about him putting his life on the line to aid one of his fellow citizens. Joy always found a way to be involved and insert himself whenever the community or unfortunate individuals needed him. In this extreme case, he ran to assist a poor

Spencer - Main Street - Spring 1931 *Before the Fire*

Main Street in Spencer prior to the fire in 1931
Clay County Heritage Center

young man who found himself in an extremely harrowing position during one of the best-known events in the history of Spencer, the Spencer fire of June 27, 1931. The Spencer fire impacted more than just Joy Roberts, of course, as the entire community came together to recover and thrive in the face of disaster.

Reading accounts of the fire that raged through the business district of Spencer that day, it is impossible not to think of scenes from modern day action movies with large explosions, towering flames, and innocents diving for cover to avoid flaming debris shooting out from the destruction in every direction imaginable. It sounds dramatic, but it is frighteningly accurate because the fire started in the worst possible place...a large sales bin full of fireworks for the upcoming Fourth of July holiday. Not surprisingly, calls for the ban of fireworks started all over Iowa as a result, but too little too late for Spencer. The city, despite the destruction of four and a half blocks of businesses along Main Street, showed amazing resilience and fortitude from the beginning. Work on rebuilding was already being reported by the local newspapers in the same weekly editions that offered the first printed accounts of the fire itself.

The fire began in the Otto Bjornstad drug store on the corner of Fourth and Main Streets. According to employees and customers of the store who witnessed the event, three young boys entered the store to purchase fireworks, and were understandably excited as most kids would be to see such a grand collection of future fun. Per city ordinances, it was the first day sales of fireworks were allowed, and the store had been advertising their largest stock of fireworks ever. The large quantities allowed them to sell fireworks at discounted prices. The advertised stock included "regular items" and cap guns at low prices, and more ominously in hindsight, one-pound skyrockets for 20 cents, and at 50 cents each, prismatic fountains and the big three-pound skyrockets.

No one seems to have known the three boys, and their identity was never discovered, or at the very least, never admitted. A small, black-haired child, presumably the youngest of the three, started the blaze. Store clerk Mary Nelson assisted the boys as they sorted through the stock for their favorites. The youngest boy somehow got a hold of a lighted punk and attempted to light a sparkler. When the sparkler lit, the boy startled and dropped it into the large bin of fireworks. Another store employee, Andrew Wahlstrom, alertly perceived the danger and tried to stop the inevitable but could not move fast enough. There was a loud bang, and the store instantly filled with flames and smoke as the rest of the stock of fireworks lit in unison. The boys, the employees in the main store, and the other customers were able to get out quickly before the store was overrun by the flames. The young boys disappeared, seemingly lost to history. There were still two employees in the store who found themselves in extremely dangerous situations.

Firefighters in Spencer racing to stop the inferno
Clay County Heritage Center

Otto Bjornstad Jr., the owner's son, worked in the prescription room on the first floor. Confused by the initial blast, it did not take long for him to realize his precarious position. The prescription room did not have a door, so before he could get his bearings, smoke and flames began pouring into the room, accompanied by what he referred to as "blinding flashes." His familiarity with the store probably saved his life. Essentially blinded by the smoke and on the verge of being overcome, he felt his way along the store counters, falling twice before reaching the cigar counter he knew to be near the front door. Making a blind rush through the heat, he made it out the door just as a new blast rocked the building. He walked down the street away from the heat and met Morgan Cornwall, who guided him out of the danger zone and provided some basic first aid with supplies from another drug store still unaffected by the fire. He survived his ordeal with minor burns around his hands, arms, head and back, and of course, some badly singed hair.

The second employee who found himself trapped in the store was John Shelmidine. He had the misfortune of being in the basement where the paint stocks were kept. When he heard the first explosion, he thought the paint stock had caught fire, by itself not a good scenario. Seeing smoke pouring into the basement by the stairs, the most obvious exit, he attempted to go through a partition in the basement wall that separated his store from the Graham department store next door. He could communicate with the other store's manager through the partition, but neither of them could break through. By that time the stairs going to the main store had collapsed, so his only option was to find the back door of the store that led to a staircase going up to the street. That is where he eventually ran into Joy Roberts.

John's journey through the smoke-filled basement did not happen quickly. The manager of Graham's, E.E. Harriman, had enough time to exit his store and solicit help from bystanders to aid in getting John out. Joy, along with Orville Kenyon and Jack Low, were aware of the staircase in back and made several efforts to get down to the door but were overcome by heat and smoke on each attempt. Finally, in desperation, John "made a blind lunge" at the back door and succeeded in breaking out and running up the steps. Joy had made three attempts to go down the stairs and suffered burns around his face. John, ironically, made it out without any injuries.

By his own admission, John Shelmidine felt fortunate to get out of the basement alive. Less than a month later, however, he must have been wondering about his luck. A small article in the Spencer Herald from July 30, sarcastically titled, "Johnny Just Can't Stay Away From Fire," recounted how he once again faced with a city-threatening fire situation. Taking a break, he and four friends drove to the Black Hills in South Dakota. One night, they rented a cabin near Hill City and were awakened in the middle of the night to be warned about a large fire threatening the campground and city. They spent the remainder of the evening assisting locals by felling trees and digging ditches to slow the approaching fire. Their efforts were rewarded, and the fire stopped prior to reaching the populated areas.

Getting back to the Spencer fire, employees and customers in Bjornstad's were not the only people in the building in immediate danger. The local phone exchange operated by the Northwestern Bell Telephone Company was located on the second floor of the building and staffed by several people. In an ironic twist, that is what led to the store owner, Otto Bjornstad Sr, learning about the fate of his building. Returning from a vacation in Wisconsin, he made a stop in Mankato, Minnesota, Saturday evening. He wanted to tell his wife he would be arriving late, so he attempted to call her. Listening to operators talk in the ensuing confusion, he overheard them say they could not connect calls to Spencer because the phone exchange had burned down. He arrived back in Spencer early the next morning to find his business a total loss.

The phone exchange was fully staffed that afternoon. There were six operators on duty under the charge of the chief operator, Marie Banning. Two small boys were at the exchange to observe the activities therein, and other staff members were in various parts of the building. After the first explosion, wire chief Sam Harris and two linemen, Kenneth Billings and Roy Eastland, moved quickly to open the second story windows and remove the screens. Harris left the exchange to get other staff members out through the main entrance. Four of the operators were ordered to leave through the front entrance as well, taking the young boys with them. Miss Banning, along with the two remaining operators, Altene Knudson and Bertha Harriman, stayed at the switchboard long enough to put in a call to the fire department.

With the proper emergency calls completed and the main entrance filled with smoke, the remaining linemen started moving the operators towards the now open window. Below in the street, a local farmer named Ernest Ferguson had run over to aid firefighters in raising a ladder to the window and climbed up himself to assist the ladies in getting down. Miss Banning got the first two operators out and followed immediately after. The two linemen were the last to exit the building. By all accounts, everyone stayed calm despite the smoke and heat. Miss Banning attributed that to the speed at which everything happened, saying there was no time to be afraid. A cameraman outside took a picture of the employees descending the ladder just three minutes after the initial blast. Miss Banning remembered her only thought as she climbed onto the ladder was to be careful not to trip.

Bjornstad Drugs, the exchange, and Graham department store were all located in the McAllister Building on the west side of Main Street, along with smaller businesses and office space. Within fifteen minutes the building was a total loss. The speed with which flames spread can be expressed by the efforts of Graham department store manager, E.E. Harriman. After alerting others to the predicament of John Shelmidine, Mr. Harriman ran to the Western Union office and sent a telegram to his company's office in Minneapolis stating, "Store next door on fire. Looks dangerous." The next telegram sent moments later summed it up. "Store gone."

The Clay County National Bank was next to the McCallister Building with the Dan Cole building next to that. All were destroyed in the fire. Surprisingly, other buildings on the block were not as badly damaged or not damaged at all. The Spencer News-Herald office directly behind Bjornstad's survived without a scratch. Most of the damage and destroyed businesses occurred on the east side of Main Street. Early problems with water pressure plagued the fire department, preventing them from getting the needed water past the second floor. Aided by a southwest wind, the flames raged to heights of one hundred feet, allowing the fire to jump the gap between the east and west sides of the street. By now, several firework displays had caught fire and the flaming projectiles shooting out of the various explosions made a bad situation even worse.

Business owners on the east side of Main Street may have had a brief hope of the fire staying on the other side, but very brief. Aware of the possibility of the fire spreading, businessman O.B. Scott decided to remove important records from his second story office. He climbed a ladder at the back of his building to avoid the heat and headed to his office. He met others rushing to the back and encouraging him to turn around and do the same. He had time to grab a briefcase and a ledger before hearing another blast and becoming surrounded by fast moving smoke and flame. The heat he said, "came as quickly as one could wink an eye." The flames were pushing forward over his head as he ran for the back door, holding his breath as he sensed the extreme danger of inhaling. He made it out of the building, but suffered significant burns to his face, hands and arms.

Many residents, including Mr. Scott, expressed frustration with the initial lack of water pressure which they felt could have prevented the fire from spreading to the east side and possibly kept the damage limited to Bjornstad's alone. It took half an hour to get the water pressure up to sufficient levels to combat the fire. Even a responding fire truck caught fire early on and had to be moved away from the emergency to allow the flames to be extinguished. With the phone exchange being one of the first buildings to be destroyed, telegrams had to be sent out requesting aid from surrounding communities. All of them responded quickly and in force, allowing the formation of a unit strong enough to get the conflagration under control.

The losses where the fire started were significantly less than on the opposite side of the street where the wind-blown flames spread quickly, and where the most intense firefighting efforts occurred. A list of total losses shows the three buildings previously mentioned on the west side, but on the east side a total of sixteen buildings were destroyed, most of which contained multiple businesses. The spread of the fire north on the west side of Main Street stalled thanks to the construction of one of the smaller buildings. Next to the Dan Cole building, which was a complete loss, stood the Kunath building. A one-story brick building made of fire-resistant materials; it provided a buffer to slow down the spread of flames, allowing firefighters to spray water down from the taller T.M. Jones and Sons building to the north. Stopping the flames at that spot allowed more resources to be diverted to the more precarious situation on the east side of Main Street.

The Cummings building, across from Bjornstad's, was the first building on the east side to catch fire. Schoeneman Bros. lumber yard was located directly behind the Cummings building. Filled with stacks of flammable materials, this would prove to be one of the areas where the hardest firefighting happened. Had the fire spread to the yard, it likely would have moved into the residential area next door. The efforts to stop the flames were successful and an even greater catastrophe averted. A similar firefight took place just north and across Mill Street from the lumberyard at the Vanderhoff service station, which also was vital in stopping movement of the fire to the east

Aerial view of the Spencer Fire
Clay County Heritage Center

Back on the east side of Main Street, the fire moved north past Fifth Street and on to Railroad Street, the next road to the north. The block between Fifth and Railroad, and between Main and Mill streets, was essentially a total loss. To finally stop the advance of the fire, dynamite was used to destroy the Spencer Dry Cleaners, creating a gap between structures. Firefighters dumped water on the gap, slowing the fire to the point that it eventually burned itself out against the brick walls of the building next door. Four hours after it started, the fire was finally extinguished, but four and a half blocks of the downtown business district were gone. Spencer, being the major commercial and business center of Clay County, suffered a substantial blow, with losses initially estimated to be around two million dollars.

Spencer proved to be extremely resilient, however, and anyone who happened to have been oblivious to the news until the next newspapers came out five days later would have seen that clearly. When the first post-fire edition of the Spencer News-Herald came out on July 2, the headline read, "Spencer Swept With $2,000,000 Fire." Directly under that, another headline read, "Rebuilding of City Already Underway." A new motto gained traction quickly, proclaiming, "We have faith in Spencer." Rebuild and rebuild better seemed to be the first instinct and some businesses began right away to seek some financial benefits. The Herald advertised the July 2 paper as a souvenir edition and encouraged locals to buy it to preserve the history of the Spencer fire. In that souvenir edition, The Medlar Studio advertised pictures of the fire for sale, encouraging customers to make their selections early from the various images available.

Local citizens and the business community stepped up immediately, and we see Joy Roberts again joining in to aid his community. Even as the flames were still burning, Mayor W.H. Lewis swore in several citizens as special police officers to help control gawking crowds and prevent looting from vulnerable businesses. Joy was among those who volunteered for the job. By Tuesday night, the Clay County National Bank became the first business to receive an insurance settlement with a payment of $25,000 for their total loss. Not all businesses were as lucky as many found themselves under insured, a hard lesson to learn. Despite it all, Spencer wasted no time in rebuilding, with a goal to have the business district up and running by the Christmas shopping season.

Just two days after the fire, the city council approved plans permitting destroyed businesses to build temporary structures to keep their operations going during the rebuilding process. The new structures were allowed for four months initially, and many businesses planned to be open by the following Monday, just over a week after the fire. By the time the July 2nd edition of the News-Herald printed, Red and Al's barber shop was already up and running; the first business to reopen. Even Bjornstad's, where the fire started, quickly began stocking up and could not wait to reopen. Over sixty telephone experts were on hand to start building a temporary telephone exchange in Spencer's former post office. As the single biggest annual event around, organizers in Spencer were quick to point out that the fire would in no way impact the Clay County Fair.

The year 1931 was already going to be significant for the fair, as construction had started on a new steel grandstand that could accommodate up to five thousand people comfortably. The fair kicked off on Tuesday, September 22, and ran through the following Saturday, September 26. The progress already made towards rebuilding the downtown area dominated conversations throughout the week, and the new grandstand succeeded as the big attraction. But while the fire did not negatively impact the fair, the same could not be said about the weather. For the first time in the fair's history there was a deficit at the end of the week. After a promising start and near record receipts early, heavy rains moved in all day on Thursday and Friday and threatened on Saturday, drowning the enthusiasm to be on the midway and other exposed attractions. The fair had always been a financial success previously, however, which provided the 1931 version with a sinking fund that easily covered the losses.

For their next goal, locals wanted to reestablish the city as the holiday shopping center for Clay County, and once again Spencer stepped up to the challenge. By the time Thanksgiving rolled around, the finishing touches were being wrapped up on the few businesses still under construction. The city planned a grand celebration to commemorate the rebuilding and recovery of the business district. Spencer celebrated its Jubilee week from December 11th through the 18th, promising great deals and treats to all who attended. Due to the sheer magnitude of the event, Santa Claus planned on spending the entire time in Spencer, occupying a special house built for the occasion. Children could drop in and talk directly with Santa, telling him everything they wanted to find under their trees while snacking on large quantities of candy. Whether or not Joy Roberts wore the red suit is uncertain. He played the role of Santa often during the 1930s, so it would make sense that he was actively involved.

Relief for the needy continued to be common theme in Spencer as always around the holidays, even when Joy did not receive any specific mention. 1931 was different though. Charitable giving continued, of course, but this year everyone wanted to celebrate recovery as well as the

15,000 People Attend Jubilee Week Finale

Crowds attending Spencer's Jubilee Week

Spencer News-Herald

resilience and fortitude of Spencer and the people who lived there. Pride in their rebuilding was the common theme throughout the month and deservedly so. The December 10th issue of the Spencer News-Herald touted the new downtown as the "district's greatest shopping center" and it seems many people came forward to spend what money they could spare. Despite the ongoing depression, Spencer businesses reported being extremely happy with their holiday profits, and the entire community celebrated their new downtown.

1931 came to a close with no updates on Joy's charitable efforts around Christmas, but he still warranted mention in a brief article on December 31. His efforts supporting and advertising the Clay County Fair were well known, and as a result the fair directors recommended Joy for a position with the Iowa exhibit at the 1933 World's Fair in Chicago. He seemed a natural fit to work in the same capacity on behalf of the entire state and when he finally made his way to Chicago, he arrived in style in what is most likely his best-known advertising gimmick, a streetcar he built himself to spread the word about the World's Greatest County Fair.

Six

Ballyhoo Man Par Excellence

The Great Depression and the resulting inability of individuals to give as generously as they had previously played a significant role in the lack of articles covering Joy's Christmas activities during the 1930s. Joy never stopped his efforts, however, and a 1947 article in the Spencer Times touched on the Depression years specifically. The article confirmed the community assistance so prevalent in aiding Joy's cause in the 1920s and later in the 1940s slowed considerably during the Depression so Joy carried out his work and the financial burden on his own. His notoriety in the press during the 1930s came primarily from his work at the Clay County Fair and on the fair's behalf around the state. At a time when people were looking for relief from their daily struggles and maybe a little levity, the fair continued to thrive.

In December 1931, the Clay County Fair's directors unanimously endorsed Joy for a position with the Iowa exhibit during the Chicago World's Fair starting in April 1933. Once approved, he would start after the 1932 Clay County Fair and be involved in promotional work. He approached his promotional work with the usual gusto, beginning at the state fair. In 1932 he and another local Spencer man, LeRoy A. Radar, were officials of racing at the state fair. Joy took on a variety of duties each year but always had a special affection for the racetrack. Radar was also the official of racing at the Clay County Fair, while Joy's duties focused on outside advertising and being the do-it-all assistant to Secretary Dailey. The press referred to Joy as Dailey's "chief aid-de-camp" and the person who fixes whatever problem may arise at the fair and eagerly anticipated his appointment to the World's Fair.

The World's Fair is a term used in the United States for large global exhibitions sanctioned since 1928 by the Bureau International des Expositions in France. In other countries the terms universal exposition or World Expo are commonly used. Between 1850 and 1938, the themes revolved around trade, technology and inventions from around the globe. In 1933, the Chicago World's Fair was officially known as A Century of Progress International Exposition and coincided with the city's centennial celebration. The official motto confirmed the focus on technological innovation... "Science Finds, Industry Applies, Man Conforms." The fair opened on May 27, 1933, and closed over a year later on October 31, 1934. In terms of the technology on display, it was hard to top the arrival of the German airship *Graf Zeppelin*, a predecessor of the ill-fated *Hindenburg* airship. While Joy could not compete with a giant airship for attention, he still managed to get a great deal of notice for his own much smaller but still unique creation.

In 1925, Joy teamed with Jimmy Sloan to create a replica of a railroad engine to advertise the Clay County Fair. The engine was designed primarily to advertise races at the fair but used for a variety of purposes. In 1932 he wanted to create something different that would be automatically associated with the fair. This time around, he teamed up with John Pruin, a caretaker at the fair for several years. The two created a replica of a big city trolley mounted on a 1919 Buick motor car chassis. As he hoped, the trolley became a symbol of the fair for several years to come, not just in Spencer, but around Iowa.

Joy and Jimmy Sloan showing off their new creation

Joy and his friends jokingly referred to his new creation as the Toonerville Trolley, and the name stuck with family over the years, but was never an official moniker. Toonerville Trolley referred to a vehicle in a well-known comic strip called Toonerville Folks that ran from 1908 to 1955 in newspapers nationwide. Joy's trolley did not need a catchy name to be recognized throughout Northwest Iowa. Known locally as the Clay County Fair streetcar, Joy made sure it became more than just a local fixture, taking it all the way to Chicago as part of his contribution to the Iowa exhibit at the World's Fair in 1933.

The streetcar was street legal and rumored to cover up to 5,000 miles a year during fair season. To add to its authenticity, the trolley boasted loudspeakers and a realistic sounding bell. Joy added a device that sent sparks flying into the air to grab even more attention. Fair scenes and advertisements were painted on the sides by Gordon Tercey, who would later move on to become an automobile designer for the Kaiser-Frazier Corporation. A full supply of postcards, placards and other items to advertise the fair were kept inside. Joy was also known to keep an extra pair of pajamas handy so he could sleep in the streetcar on his journeys to ensure an early start each day.

The first mention of the streetcar found in local newspapers appeared on August 25, 1933, announcing that Joy had taken his newly created toy to Des Moines where he was working at the Iowa State Fair, and using his spare time to advertise. The article called Joy the "chief of fair boosters and ballyhoo man par excellence." He would drive through the fairgrounds playing music and promoting the glory of the Clay County Fair. His work at the state fair usually had something to do with racing, so taking advantage of his position, he planned to get the streetcar in front of the grandstand "by hook or by crook." There is no record of whether he succeeded or not.

His "by hook or by crook" approach did get him some free advertising on occasion and his fast talking got him out of trouble. In 1960, a local reporter wrote an article reminiscing about one of Joy's advertising coups. Just prior to the state fair one year, he learned of a parade put on by Des Moines businessmen and as usual saw an opportunity. Joy managed to insert himself and his streetcar into the parade mid-route. Local police stopped him and asked why he was there. He told them he had become stuck in parade traffic and could not find a way out. They allowed him to continue. In the same article, local resident Roy LaBrant remembered, "He could get himself in with advertising where no other human could." That seems to be a very accurate memory.

Joy and the streetcar began making rounds in Spencer when his work at the state fair concluded. Tickets for that year's Clay County Fair were about to go on sale at the fair office. For those who were unable to purchase tickets during regular fair office hours, Joy would be selling them from the streetcar on Saturday nights. He parked his mobile office on Main Street and true to his personality, he would put on a show. This would be his normal strategic sales location in Spencer for several years. Another article from 1941, during the weeks leading up to the fair of course, told how Joy stationed himself outside the mayor's office in his streetcar giving "blow-by-blow" reports on traffic conditions to all weekend shoppers within range of his loudspeakers.

The county fair was scheduled for September 19 to 23 in 1933. For several weeks prior to the start of the fair, Joy's "famous" streetcar toured around Northwest Iowa to ensure no one forgot about the excitement to come. He kept it up during the fair days, and at the end of the week, received four offers to use the streetcar for other advertising ventures. The auto racing association, carnival company and a few other companies who operated at the fair extended the offers, and Joy considered applying for a copyright for use of the streetcar as an advertising medium. Whether he followed up on the copyright idea is not known. The offers from the various companies were all turned down because Joy had a bigger prize in mind. He was taking his streetcar to the Chicago World's fair.

Joy made the trip to Chicago on his own time, but all expenses were paid for by the fair association who clearly saw value in the publicity. The streetcar joined a large Iowa contingent participating in the American Legion's national convention parade on October 3. The Iowa section included 20,000 Iowans carrying cornstalks to give the impression of a moving cornfield. Somewhere, either at the beginning or end of the cornfield, Joy would drive his streetcar in front of the crowds enjoying the spectacle. The parade went down Michigan Avenue and concluded on the grounds of the World's Fair. The streetcar had the desired effect even in a large city like Chicago, attracting a crowd wherever it went. Joy was quoted as saying, "A streetcar seems more of a novelty in Chicago than any place else and we had difficulty going through the jams around it on several occasions."

The true novelty, however, was the trip itself. It would be quite an accomplishment in the streetcar and Joy made a point to plan the trip to achieve maximum visibility. He took his two children along for the ride. Charles, who also went by Bud or Buddy at times, was seventeen years old and starting his senior year in high school. Joyce, now Joyce James, was married and had a young son, Charles Dean James, who presumably stayed with his grandmother while the others went off to Chicago. Almost a year and a half old at the time, Dean would eventually spend a considerable amount of time as a young teenager assisting Joy in his many Christmas endeavors.

The trio may have followed Joy's routine of camping in the streetcar at times, but it was a long trip, and an occasional hotel stay would be understandable. All said, they traveled 1,200 miles on their round trip, taking different routes there and back to cover as much ground as possible. On the way to Chicago, they headed east to Mason City and then dropped slightly south to pass through Waterloo, Dubuque and Rockford, Illinois. On the return trip they took the Lincoln Highway which ran just south of the previous route, passing through or near Clinton, Cedar Rapids and Ames, before turning north back to Spencer. As in Chicago, the streetcar attracted large crowds at each stop. Building on Joy's usual Northwest Iowa circuit, his journey though Eastern and Central Iowa offered a whole new potential audience for future fairs. When he and his kids returned, the streetcar was stored away for the winter to avoid the potential ravages of Iowa's sometimes harsh cold season.

Over the next several years, the streetcar continued to be a regular sight during the buildup to the fair. The usual routine started with a trip to the state fair, followed by the circuit around Northwest Iowa, and the regular stops on Saturday nights in downtown Spencer selling grandstand and season tickets. Mabry Cornwall helped Joy with maintenance and upkeep and sometimes assisted with driving duties. The streetcar made those annual rounds through 1941 but stopped during the war years from 1942 and 1945. Why it stopped being used during those years is unclear, but the streetcar made a short post-war comeback in 1946 before being officially retired. An article from 1949 boasted that the streetcar had been "as much a symbol of the fair as the gates to the grounds themselves."

The 1949 article was sadly symbolic in a way. Written less than a year after Joy passed away, it showed a picture of the dilapidated trolley. The frame had been found in a back corner of the fairgrounds in an advanced state of disrepair. The streetcar did not fade from local memory though. Another pre-fair article in 1967 stated boldly that the fair owed a great deal of gratitude to Joy for starting an advertising program that had continued successfully ever since. A separate pamphlet said Joy "is the continuous thread woven through the Clay County Fair project from the beginning until his death." The same pamphlet quoted former secretary Leo Dailey as saying Joy put his "heart and soul in the fair."

The Clay County Fair streetcar was easily the most visible symbol of that commitment.

There were still no references to Joy's Christmas activities following his trip to the World's Fair in 1933. He did make news in 1934 when he jumped into the political fray one more time. This time, instead of running for mayor, he entered the Democratic primary race for the area's state representative. Now forty-five years old and in his tenth year as a local insurance agent, his bio in the local paper skimmed over some of those mundane facts and focused on his more visible accolades. His duties at the Clay County and state fairs were listed, of course, and his advertising using his streetcar highlighted. No one mentioned him using the streetcar to push his own political aspirations, and that may have been frowned upon by the fair in any case. He was touted as Spencer's official Santa Claus and given credit for playing Santa for various organizations over the previous twenty-three years.

Joy's bio recalled his previous history of campaigning for mayor but was not entirely accurate. It claimed his run for mayor in 1926 had been his only foray into politics, forgetting about his first attempt at the same office in 1924. In 1926, he started the race but dropped out of his own accord to attend to his insurance business. He still managed one vote. In an odd sidenote, he claimed to have been a faithful Democrat for twenty-four years, except in 1932. That year he "entered" a Republican political primary but does not appear to have been a candidate. He may have supported a Republican, and later that year he supported Herbert Hoover in the presidential election against Franklin D. Roosevelt. Maybe that is what drove him back to the Democratic party, because in the first election since the start of the Great Depression, Roosevelt defeated Hoover in an electoral landslide, 472 to 59.

His political advertisements lacked the same flair as his fair efforts. An ad prior to the election announced the office he was running for and rather blandly stated, "Your support is earnestly solicited." Clay County at the time seemed to be staunchly Republican. The incumbent for the office was a Republican and running without competition in his primary. The Democratic primary had four candidates, and newspapers speculated that the turnout would be higher than normal. Previous primaries had been small affairs generating maybe 150 to 200 votes, but it was hoped that having several candidates to choose from would lift that number as high as 400 to 500. In the end, 669 votes were tallied. Joy ended up the low man of the four, however, bringing in just 89 votes.

Joy never ran for political office after that, choosing instead to stick with what he did best. He quickly moved on to his usual roles at the local fairs. He once again served as assistant superintendent of speed at the state fair and as head of advertising for the county fair. Joy was not the only member of his family showing ambitions that year, however. His son, Charles, actively served in his local DeMolay organization. DeMolay is a youth leadership organization often sponsored by Masonic groups, of which Joy was an active member. The DeMolays strove to teach young people leadership traits through community service and fundraising. In April, while Joy campaigned for the state representative office, Charles was named District Senior Councilor of the local Spencer chapter. After graduating from high school in June, he followed up that success in December, being elected the Senior Master Councilor of the Order of DeMolay at a conclave that included DeMolays from six local cities.

Less than a month after being elected, Charles found himself the center of attention again, but in considerably less desirable circumstances. He brought the new year in at the University hospital in Iowa City, having been diagnosed with cervical ribs. A cervical rib is a rare condition where an extra set of ribs grows from the sides of the seventh cervical vertebrae which is the next vertebrae up from where the ribs usually start. It is a rare condition, affecting less than one percent of the population, and does not always lead to symptoms. In Charles' case though, the extra ribs grew under his collar bone and came into contact with the nerves in his arms, causing pain in his neck and arms. In addition to the pain, cervical ribs can lead to other conditions with much more serious consequences.

Once in Iowa City, Charles became a bit of a celebrity with several leading surgeons at the hospital wanting to perform the operation. In 1935 with medical advancements not what they are today, the surgery to correct cervical ribs was a rare occurrence and

Joy and Lena Roberts in 1936

not without some risks. At the time the hospital only had a total of eleven similar cases previously. However the surgeons agreed to divvy up the duties, the surgery was a success and by the time the local Spencer papers shared the story, Charles was well on his way to recovery.

For the next three years, the only references to Joy or his family in the newspapers were the usual reports about his activities at the Clay County Fair and its summer build up. In 1935, Joy and his assistants LaVern Jones and Hugh Richards were said to be "buzzing madly about the grounds all week." In 1936, he served as the general manager and superintendent of privileges, and in 1937 he oversaw management of the grounds and, of course, outside advertising.

At the end of 1937 Joy finally found himself back in the local newspapers in his usual role as either Santa Claus or, in this case, Santa's advanced booking agent. Other than a brief reference to Joy dressing as Santa in 1934 for a community event, he had not been mentioned in a Christmas role since 1928. As the effects of the Great Depression slowly diminished, he saw his visibility as Spencer's Santa return along with charitable giving from the community. The 1937 article was brief but showed a full dive back into Christmas activities for Joy. He announced that Santa would be spending an entire week in Spencer but did more than just act as Santa's agent that week. He played the role of Dark Sam in a local production of Dicken's Christmas Carol. Asked about his acting, we get a rare quote on how he viewed his role as Santa Claus when he told a local reporter, "Santa's role is one where the actor has more real pleasure than the audience."

In the same article, when discussing Santa's arrival in a sleigh, there is a reference that would make no sense under normal circumstances. To quote the article, "Mr. Roberts was unable to state whether the toy sleigh would be drawn by reindeer or coons but it's of little matter as long as the toys get here." Why would raccoons pulling a sleigh even be considered a possibility? The answer can be found in some family pictures showing Joy holding two raccoons while standing on the sidewalk in downtown Spencer. In one picture that looks like a lost advertising gimmick, one of the raccoons is happily drinking soda from a glass bottle. Where and how and for how long Joy had the raccoons is unknown, but they were another means to hang out on Main Street and start conversations with strangers in hopes of finding out what children wanted for Christmas and what families were in need.

Joy and his raccoons getting the attention of curious children

There are not many references to the raccoons, but one of the more enthusiastic came from an interview in 1995. As part of a video series designed to create an oral history of Spencer by interviewing long-term citizens, Janice Orr interviewed Ben Shine. Mr. Shine, fifty years later, had vivid memories of Joy and still thought highly of him. "E. Joy Roberts," he said, "from father to son will always be remembered in Spencer." His quotes speak for themselves, so they are presented here in full.

"I will tell you one of the things I'll always remember as a boy. We can talk about the leading citizens of Spencer. Most of 'em they talk about is financially. I'll tell you about a little leading citizen of Spencer...E. Joy Roberts, because he would always pick up toys and rebuild toys for Christmas time for kids."

And he did remember the raccoons...

"Toys! Making toys for the children. Oh...he had the toys for children. I can still see him walking down the street. He always had a raccoon on his shoulder. All the dogs was trying to get the raccoon, I think. But he was an outstanding citizen, I think. From the heart, E. Joy Roberts was outstanding."

Ben Shine's interview points to memories specific to the late 1930's. Not only because of the reference to the raccoons, but also due to his references to Joy collecting and rebuilding toys for children. Joy's practice of making and refurbishing toys had been mentioned in local newspapers from time to time but became a focal point starting in 1938 as his Christmas activities began to take center stage again. Joy partnered with the Eagles Lodge to create a toy clinic where he would work with local youths to repair and touch up old toys that could then be used to provide Christmas gifts for boys and girls who might otherwise go without. On December 8 an appeal went out in the Spencer Times to children and parents who were willing to donate toys that were no longer needed or in danger of being thrown out. The hope was that this program would grow and become a permanent annual event. It did continue and would become the charitable act Joy would be most known for going forward.

Two weeks after the first article, both local newspapers put out calls for even more toys to be donated. Working from a workshop referred to as the "Santa Claus house" on West Pine Street, Joy and his helpers prepared 178 toys for distribution on Christmas day, but more were needed to meet local needs and time was running out. They were well prepared to work quickly. The workshop had been set up by the Eagles who purchased full sets of tools along with lathes, saws and various other power tools to ensure the program had everything it needed to succeed. Donated items did not need to be dropped off as locals could call the shop or the Eagles Lodge, and arrangements would be made to send someone to pick up the soon to be "new" gifts.

The newspapers did a good job reintroducing the public to Joy's previous holiday exploits. Now Santa Claus to a second generation of young people in Clay County, he would occasionally draw from his 24-year-old collection of letters to Santa to remind young adults of wishes they had made when they were younger. According to the new articles, he had been playing the part of Santa in the Spencer business district since 1920, again verifying the suspicion that he regularly wore the red suit during the 1930s even though his charitable acts were not followed in the local press. Joy insisted he had no plans to slow down on his toy repair duties after Christmas but would continue through the winter months and beyond so there would be an abundance of toys ready next year, hoping to avoid last-minute pleas for more.

On December 29, 1938, the Spencer Daily Reporter shared a picture of Joy standing behind a stack of toys in his workshop on Christmas Eve. Later that day he and his helpers went out in the community to distribute the joyous bounty. The last line in the caption perfectly captures the sentiment after Christmas. "Many children in this territory were gladdened by the visit from Santa Claus they hardly dared hope for." True to his words, Joy started right in preparing for the next Christmas season, and the number of children reached highlighted the fruits of that labor.

The following year, 406 toys were given out to 221 children. Joy's early preparations also allowed him to provide over 80 toys throughout 1939 to children from poorer families who were sick. Going forward, he was never alone in his efforts. Brothers Beryl and Leslie Jones aided Joy in his repair work on a regular basis. In a different article, the Jones brothers were referred to as Laverne and Vearl, and over the years Laverne went by Lee. For the sake of consistency, we will refer to him as Lee as that was the most common name local newspapers used when his role as Joy's assistant increased. Lee remained a constant presence for several years in Joy's toy shops. Mrs. Cuttell made new dresses for old dolls and helped put new outfits on them. Mabry Cornwall, who helped Joy with upkeep on his streetcar from time to time, assisted while home from school at Dartmouth. Joy was sponsored as usual by the Spencer Eagles.

As part of the Christmas fundraising efforts, the Eagles arranged an after-school movie at the Spencer Theater on December 5. Admission could be a new or used toy which would be turned over to Joy and his team. The Eagles also donated money for dolls, which had been an item of need the previous year. Other groups and agencies eagerly provided assistance as well. The Methodist Ladies Aid provided several items, the city recreation department staff made wooden toys of their own to donate, and the county welfare agency gave several toys after their own distribution to rural children was complete. As a result of this generous giving and plans to continue in the future, Joy's workshop was overwhelmed.

The workshop, more accurately just a small shed, sat behind the Roberts home. In addition to the tools and toys being worked on, the shop doubled as a place to store parts from toys that were unable to be salvaged. Those parts were saved for future repairs. As more donations rolled in, the small shop became woefully inadequate. As a result, completed toys were stored in a room in the Roberts house to await distribution. A reporter who was given access noted that there was hardly any room to stand. "A large davenport was literally buried by dolls, in one corner were hundreds of toy airplanes and cars, in another was games, and in still another mechanical toys. Outside on the porch were sleds, tricycles and other larger articles." The need for a bigger shop was obvious and because many children on Joy's list were also on the list receiving county aid, some officials considered providing financial assistance to make it happen.

Ready to go for Christmas 1939
Spencer Daily Reporter

That would be a topic to be discussed at another time, however, as the focus turned to the distribution of toys. In an extremely rare turn of events, Joy could not personally deliver the toys. He developed a severe cold and had to sit that year out, but Mabry Cornwall and Vearl Jones stepped in to make sure needy children of Spencer and Clay County received the gifts that had been so diligently prepared for them. The task of getting toys to so many children took up all day on both Christmas Eve and Christmas. By the time the local newspapers reported on that year's giving, Joy began soliciting donations for the next. The 1930s, which had started so quietly in the press despite Joy's continuous giving throughout, ended strong and his reputation as Spencer's Santa grew. As the 1940s began and Joy embarked on his fourth decade in that role, the community and the local press would help carry his work to even greater heights.

Seven

Spencer's Spirit of Christmas

In the 1940s, almost all the articles about Joy Roberts focused on his Christmas activities. There were no more political aspirations, his children were grown, and even though he stayed active with the fair, there were no more grand inventions to match the Clay County Fair streetcar. There are pictures of the streetcar showing the 1946 fair dates, the year it made a brief comeback, but no feature articles. Early in the 1940s, the Christmas coverage was consistent but not overdone. That all changed in 1946 when local newspapers not only went all in on current stories about Joy but also began telling his life story and passing it along to larger newspapers in Des Moines and beyond.

In 1940, the newspapers found time to cover Joy and his toy drives, but the main headlines and majority of space were dominated by the war in Europe. Americans were nervous and anticipating US entry into the war, and it would indeed be the last Christmas before that happened. Children on the other hand were not likely to understand the complexities of war, and Joy refused to allow even rumors of war to keep him from his mission for the needy children in Spencer. The Eagles Lodge remained ready to assist to ensure the needs of local children were met and their dreams of Santa Claus were uninterrupted.

The now annual movie at the Fraser Theater, where children received free admission with the donation of a new or used toy, continued as the main fundraising event. Scheduled for Tuesday, the show began at 4pm to ensure children had time to get there after a long day of school. While the show did not bring in as many toys as the year before, the Daily Reporter felt the toys were of much better quality than in the past. When all the toys were collected, Joy had them transported to his new toy shop in the basement of Buddie's Waffle Shop. Buddie, of Buddie's Waffle Shop, was Joy's son Charles who went by Buddie most of his adult life. The waffle shop was one of his early forays into business.

The public was again invited to come in and tour the toy shop and always encouraged to bring toys when they did. Joy would also take cash donations to assist with purchasing paint and other supplies required to properly restore toys to good working order. The newspaper shared a picture showing Joy hard at work with his assistants Lee Jones and Don Noehren restoring old toys. Local businesses also donated toys, and Sears Roebuck gave an especially generous donation when the local office donated all their toy samples to Joy when the Christmas shopping season ended just prior to the holiday. The coverage of Joy focused almost exclusively on his toys and shop, adding more to the rumors that Joy may in fact be Santa Claus.

On December 4, 1941, the Spencer Times, the more locally oriented of the two newspapers in Spencer, shared an article about Joy meeting with members of the Spencer Woman's Club at the Spencer Library. They had a Christmas tree set up with a pile of wrapped presents underneath. Joy attended the meeting to give an account to the ladies in attendance regarding his charitable efforts and how he went about planning and distributing gifts to the less fortunate. He had a list of 293 children who may need assistance along with their families and gave his usual appeal for more toys. In response, the gifts under the tree were opened and the toys they contained were donated to Joy on the spot.

On that same day, the more nationally focused Spencer Reporter's front page focused mainly on news of the ongoing war in Europe. It should be common knowledge, of course, that three days later the United States entered the war following the Japanese attack on Pearl Harbor. Af-

From the current family collection, a toy car repaired and painted in Joy's toy shop

ter December 7 the headlines predictably shifted to the new reality of a war that had become personal. On December 16 and 20 the focus continued to be almost exclusively on the war, but they did not forget Joy. On both days the Reporter placed small articles on the front-page giving updates on his work. It was the standard fare, with Joy asking for more toy donations and for help with dressing the large number of dolls he had collected that needed repair or at least a new outfit. His toy shop moved to a new location in the Rite-Way Cleaners building and the public as always was invited to take a tour.

On December 27, instead of the usual post-Christmas follow up, newspapers reported that Joy had been selected as the chairman of the Roosevelt Birthday Ball committee, tasked with planning various events around the county to celebrate the sixtieth birthday of President Franklin D. Roosevelt. All funds raised by the events would be donated to the National Foundation Against Infantile Paralysis. It sounds somewhat ironic considering Joy admitted during one of his political campaigns to have switched loyalty temporarily to the Republican party in 1932, the same year Roosevelt was elected to his first term as president. At the end of 1941, he appears to have had a change of heart and fully embraced the president and his war effort.

The newspaper articles in 1942 struck many familiar tunes. The movie at the Fraser Theater brought in an abundance of toy donations to fill Joy's workshop which was once again located in the Rite-Way Cleaners building. Visitors were welcome to come to the shop, even more so if they were willing to work on dressing the refurbished dolls piling up. The only unique news recounted a Christmas party held by the Eagles in which Joy himself "burst forth in a brand-new suit for the occasion" as Santa Claus instead of simply being Santa's assistant. When his Christmas rounds were complete, Joy had delivered 411 toys to 179 children. He asked the Spencer Daily Reporter to express his thanks to his many donors and volunteers, making special mention of Jessie McArdle, Lee Jones, Don Noehren, Mr. Bartrom, and his grandson, Dean James.

Joy's grandson, Dean, now eleven years old, would become a regular in the toy shop as he entered his teenage years. During the early part of World War II, Dean's mother, Joyce, moved to Washington DC to work in the Navy Department so Dean lived with Joy and Lena. While working in DC, Joyce met Roscoe Fertick who also worked in the Navy Department as an active-duty cryptologist. The two were married and soon afterward welcomed their only child together, Roscoe Jr., on June 14, 1943. Just days later, Dean accompanied another local serving in the War Department,

Margaret Schuldt, back to DC to meet his new brother. Roscoe Jr. would spend much of his youth in Spencer and could often be found in the toy shop, too young to help, but usually with a look of wide-eyed wonder to be in such a treasure-filled room as a toddler.

During the Christmas season of 1943, Joy continued his work as always, but the Spencer Reporter focused not only on what Joy did for others, but on what the community could do for Joy. They reminded readers that Joy had been doing his good work for thirty years and had "constituted himself into a special kind of Santa Claus—a Santa Claus for those children who would otherwise be disappointed." They estimated that over the years he had spent $4,000 of his own money and given away 6,500 gifts. Joy announced his desire to build a workshop in his backyard. He would still have his headquarters in rooms downtown for the public side of his work but needed space for the tools he had collected over the years and his stacks of spare parts. The Reporter wanted to take the lead helping Joy get his workshop and began soliciting readers in mid-November to give to what they considered "the vanguard of all worthy causes in the entire community."

Donations were coming in before the announcement was officially made. The Eagles Lodge and several individuals had given money, and the Stolley Gravel Company donated gravel for the foundation and floor. While Joy was asking for assistance with dressing his numerous dolls once more, the community continued to assist him with both his giving and his workshop. More local businesses wanted to get in on the generosity. Ole Dickson offered to do any welding work on toys for free, and with the floor of the toy shop ready to go, H&S Modernizing Firm donated the necessary roofing supplies. Local radio station KICD gave Joy free airtime on Saturday and Sunday prior to Christmas to tell the community about his work on a show they called the Joy Roberts Santa Claus Program.

In the end it was an overwhelming community effort. Not satisfied with only giving their money, two local men started a petition in Spencer and raised $119 with their solicitations. Joy's holiday activities also began to attract attention outside of Clay County and even outside of Iowa. He received a $10 donation from an anonymous donor in California and $15 from New Orleans. In the end, Joy raised a total of $473.50 and reported that the giving of toys and dolls made it the largest response he had ever received in his thirty years as Santa Claus. The Reporter praised the community for what it called "a fine response to the appeal."

The most touching donations came from parents who lost their sons in the war. Joy always showed a heart for soldiers in the two world wars he lived through, so these donations would have touched him deeply. The first donation of $10 came anonymously from a local family who had set up a memorial fund in honor of their son. The second was the donation from New Orleans. Major R.A. Peterson donated $15 "in memory of my son, Bus, who gave his life in the cause that this world can continue to be a free and happy one for future generations." The generosity of those grieving parents provided a stark reminder of the sorrow going on overseas and in the homes of families who lived in constant fear for their loved ones amid the otherwise joyous season.

In 1944 Joy had his two workshops. The shop in his yard with tools for heavy work and painting, and the shop at Rite-Way Cleaners for lighter work and where he invited the public to come in to help with doll dresses and repairs that did not require his larger tools. The public was always invited to come in for a look around and often encouraged to stay and help. Joy added a new offer that year. Parents with toys they wanted to repair for their own children were invited to come to his shops and use his equipment, and he would show them how to do the work if necessary. That would come in handy as many toys were not available that year, a likely result of the ongoing war where supplies were needed and the public made sacrifices when they could, as with the meatless and sweetless days mentioned during Joy's World War I efforts.

Just before Christmas, the Daily Reporter offered some insights into how Joy's Christmas rounds were accomplished. Boxes for needy families were loaded into two cars that would cover all of Clay County, including the cities of Dickens, Webb, Greenville, Peterson, Royal, Everly and of course, Spencer. The boxes were labeled by family, taking advantage of Joy's always up to date knowledge of the names and ages of the children. In some cases, there were eleven children in a household. Each child would get two or three toys, usually with one significant toy and a couple smaller items. The rounds were made on Christmas Eve, and toys were

Joy in 1944 sitting in his very crowded toy shop

given to mothers who could hand them out on Christmas morning. The list of volunteers that year included the ever-present Don Noehren, Lee Jones and Dean James, along with Howard Kabrick, Clarence Kabrick, Dickie Kennaston and Dickie Flier.

In 1945, the war mercifully ended. Joy had been doing his part, using his unmatched fundraising and advertising skills in the war effort. Prior to starting his holiday work, he spent several weeks working in Des Moines for the National War Fund and the Iowa War Chest, tasked with organizing war relief overseas and various other patriotic duties. Not surprisingly, his toy shop that year was in the basement of the War Activities office. He made his annual appeal for toys and emphasized that any state of disrepair was acceptable. "Don't throw away a thing. Let me throw it away." Even if a toy was deemed irreparable, the parts could always be put to good use.

Joy needed no last-minute rush or appeals for more money that year. By December 15 he reported that most of his prep work was already complete and began to appeal for the names of more underprivileged children in the unlikely chance there were some who were not yet on his list. "I don't want to miss a single child," he said, and he thanked everyone who had helped him so ably in his preparations. Instead of two separate cars, Joy made his deliveries in a truck donated by Fred Wadsley, assisted by his grandson Dean, Mr. Chesley and Bobbie Jones.

In 1946 Joy had been working as an insurance man for nearly twenty-five years, and while there were a few mentions of it here and there over the years, his other activities always overshadowed his day job. He may have worked from home at times, but that year he had his own office across from the post office with his Christmas headquarters located underneath in the basement. The proximity to his collection of old toys made it easy to combine efforts, and clients entering his office often found him with a toy or two on his desk, making repairs and prepping for the upcoming holiday. Unlike the previous year when he was ready by mid-December, on December 14 he said he had been working mostly alone that year. Money was not an issue as he had generous donations from the Eagles Lodge and the Junior Chamber of Commerce, but he could always use manpower.

The help came as it usually did...better late than never. Local boy scouts offered their assistance in the toy shop and by the next update on December 19 the newspapers reported seeing lights in his office late into the night as Jessie McCartle and Don Noehren stayed up with Joy for the last-minute preparations. By the time December 23 rolled around, Joy praised the amount of help he received from local organizations and local businesses, as well as generous giving from the public. He even received a brand-new paint machine to make his work easier, donated by Bob MacDowell. He would have seventy-eight stops on his Christmas rounds, so he wisely split up the duties.

The first rounds were completed on December 23 by Bill Chesley, accompanied by Dean James and Dickie Underwood. The trio of helpers were responsible for forty-eight deliveries around the county. They had a lot of gifts to carry as just one of those families was getting twenty-eight packages of various sizes. The Daily Reporter said it simply. "There are many children in that family." The volunteers used a "secret route" to get the gifts to parents since deliveries were on the 23rd and needed to be hidden prior to Christmas morning. Joy and his crew made the rounds to thirty households in Spencer on Christmas Eve.

1946 started like any other year for Joy in Spencer but became increasingly notable as the holiday season progressed. New, larger news organizations began noticing and paying attention to his activities. Local coverage of Joy's Christmas giving seemed as familiar to residents of Clay County as advertisements of sales in local stores. That Christmas, however, the Des Moines Register sent a reporter to interview the man familiar for his work at the state fair, hoping to learn more about the legend growing around his role as the Spencer Santa Claus. The children of Spencer truly believed Joy Roberts was Santa, and the Register wanted the rest of the state to discover why.

Joy always insisted that he acted only as Santa's helper, but not everyone believed it, nor did they want to believe it. The children of Spencer, according to the Register, recognized Santa as "a slight figure in a business suit, wearing a lop-sided felt hat, driving an eight-year-old car named Emma Jean." They knew he worked as an insurance salesmen, and maybe that just added to the mystery. Children were familiar with his house where loose toys covered the front porch and the toy shop in back buzzed with curious activities. They also knew letters to Santa were delivered directly to the same house. He could insist all he wanted that Santa Claus lived at the North Pole, but would have a hard time convincing his young, local admirers.

The article claimed Joy had delivered over 14,000 toys to children during his thirty-four-year crusade. He recalled how early on he made his deliveries in a sleigh, fully decked out in his Santa costume. There were descriptions of his house, his office, and the toy shop at home, described as his garage but never used for that purpose. The descriptions matched the observations of local children...toys and tools everywhere, even inside the house where the reporter was given access children wished for but could not see from the outside. Letters sent to the house were shown off, including some that were addressed to "Joyland."

Joy explained how he went about creating his own list. There were letters, of course, informing him of needy children or received from needy children themselves. He maintained contact with county welfare agencies and various organizations he worked with over the years. He no longer had his raccoons so he would patrol the streets with a pocket full of peanuts to offer in exchange for a conversation about children who might be in need. He would also talk to local parents in secret about what their children wanted, and his covert knowledge would convince the children even more that their Santa Claus clearly knew what was in their hearts. The article said Joy's list provided him with information on good boys and girls, but he never put much thought into good or bad, just needs.

A family hard at work. Joy and Lena with their grandsons Dean James and Roscoe Fertick Jr.

Joy provided rare insights into techniques he used when playing Santa Claus on those occasions where he personally donned the red suit. He would observe Santas in various locales to see how they portrayed the generous saint. He saw it as a rare art, and in his case, he put real emphasis on the art portion. He lamented that most Santas "don't work hard enough at the part or give the children sufficient credit for seeing through the crude prater and poor disguises." We already mentioned his preference for tight whiskers and forgoing the fake belly. His insistence that children are smarter than most adults give them credit for likely went a long way towards the trust and confidence they had in believing he was the real deal.

Joy had an answer to every child's question. He would often come by car, but only because there was not always enough snow for a sleigh to operate. The rumor that Santa Claus came down the chimney could not be true because not all houses have fireplaces. Santa, as it turns out, has a master set of keys for every house and knows how to come through windows from the outside even if they are locked. The children did not need to worry. Santa Claus would always find a way in. His amazing ability to know the names of children was as simple as listening down the line to conversations between children and their parents all while talking to the child on his lap at that moment. Attention to detail and the ability to multitask were key. Sometimes both the children and the parents were surprised at how much Santa knew before they got to him.

The article in the Des Moines Register included the same story recounted earlier about the year twelve-year-old Charles had doubts about whether Santa Claus was real, leading to his mother, Lena, stating that Santa may be called by many names, including Joy Roberts. The family kept the article, and it eventually ended up in the box where the original treasure trove of information about Joy was found. The old, original newspaper clipping is in rough shape but tells a story that inspired when rediscovered by his family and was inspirational to many in Iowa when it originally printed. That year saw Joy's story reach a significantly larger audience, and that would continue the following year when the Des Moines Associated Press sent another reporter to Spencer to continue and expand their coverage from the previous Christmas.

When the new article appeared on December 19, 1947, it summarized the information shared the previous year with a few current quotes and comments added to keep it fresh. The goal was not to give new insights into Joy's work but to maximize the audience reached. The editor's note that preceded the article read, "The following story written by Jack Erickson of the Des Moines Associated Press staff was transmitted over the wires of this news service today. A wire photo supplemented the story. The Spencer Daily Reporter is happy to have cooperated with Erickson in preparing this story and bringing it to the millions of newspaper readers." Joy's story was about to be introduced to a much larger audience, but he was still Spencer's own, and the local papers were not going to take a backseat in celebrating their local hero.

The Spencer newspapers wasted little time espousing Joy's cause that year. The Spencer Times got off to a quick start with a feature article about Joy in early November and on November 13 their second article praised the involvement of the Junior Chamber of Commerce. Known as the Jaycees, the Junior Chamber of Commerce donated $50 that year just as they had in 1946. Their involvement in 1947 was significant and with the benefit of hindsight, would have a lasting impact. It was a banner year for Joy and his work. There were no shortages of donations or toys, and the community efforts must have made Joy's heart glad. With the

Jaycees, he may not have known it, but he was seeing the beginning of the continuance of his legacy after he was gone. They honored Joy with their efforts that year and continue to honor his memory with their efforts in his name to this day.

The $50 donation from the Jaycees was just the beginning. They formed a committee that included Dr. D.P. Schmitt, Joe Scolock, Allen Coughenour, and Wayne Hurd to investigate the possibility of securing a workshop for Joy in downtown Spencer. He still had room in his garage, his home, his office, and the office basement for storage and toy repairs, but this would be a location where the public could once again view Santa at work and drop off donations. It would be the headquarters for the Joy Roberts Fund. The committee's first inquiry considered a building located at the Clay County Fairground, owned by Peerless Chick Hatchery. The imagination runs wild on this one as it is hard not to imagine a structure much like a chicken coop, but the offer did not go through, and the Jaycees continued to look elsewhere for an appropriate home for Santa Claus.

A week later, efforts to find an existing building small enough to move to the desired location were still coming up empty. By December 4, the committee changed course and decided the Jaycees would build a prefabricated workshop for Joy themselves. Time was of the essence, because Santa and Mrs. Claus were scheduled to arrive in Spencer on December 13. The workshop would be open every afternoon from December 13 to Christmas Eve, and on several evenings as Christmas got closer. Parents would be able to bring their children in to watch Santa, "locally known as Joy Roberts," repairing toys and getting them ready for his annual Christmas Eve trip around the county.

Returning to November, the pending visit from old Saint Nick meant a lot of prep work needed to happen to get ready. The Spencer Times included an insert on November 20 showing a picture of Santa Claus in a crowded workshop telling readers, "Don't throw that toy away...GIVE IT TO 'JOY.' He repairs them, paints them...and distributes them to needy children of Clay County at Christmas time. Donate to the 'Joy' Roberts Christmas Fund." He would have plenty of help. The Spencer

Don't throw that toy away...
GIVE IT TO "JOY"

He Repairs Them
Paints them . . . and distributes them
to needy children of Clay county at
Christmas time. Donate to the "Joy"
Roberts Christmas Fund.

Give it to Joy!
Spencer Times

Flyers Club set up donation "depots" for toys, cash, and clothing at several locations in Spencer, as well as Milford, Hartley and Ruthven. Emmetsburg and Estherville also wanted to have their own donation boxes. The superintendent of Spencer Schools announced that local schools would participate in the collection of broken toys.

Joy reveled in the changes he had seen from his first year as Santa in 1913 to 1947. He always enjoyed repairing old toys rather than spending money, but during those early years he had to buy a lot of items to keep up. His collection of used toys had not grown to the level he enjoyed later in life. As that collection grew over the years, his appeals changed from asking for money to asking for more castoff toys. He could still get toys from local sources and never turned them down, but he did not need to use his own money to buy them anymore. With more donations coming in, however, he could if he wanted to. When asked as Christmas approached if he had enough toys, he proudly proclaimed, "We always have enough toys. We clear out the great stock in the workshop and storerooms. If we need more, we get them. There are always toys as long as there is one left in Spencer stores."

Joy had a huge list of needy children by now, but that did not stop him from looking for more. The Daily Reporter understood that Joy still felt being overlooked on Christmas "is just about the saddest event that can happen to any boy and girl." The community felt the same and their outpouring of help was as generous as ever. Several women assisted with dressing the dolls. Joy praised generous contributions coming in the mail from as far away as Florida. Lee Jones and Don Noehren were still ever-present assistants in the workshop and Joy never missed an opportunity to praise his grandson, Dean, for his help. "He has been helping me ever since he was old enough."

Joy's workshop was a model of efficiency. He had all the tools and helpers he needed and an abundance of discarded toys to repair. Joy strove for quality. He wanted to restore the toys to as close to new conditions as possible. The Daily Reporter praised what it called "an ingenious method of using wooden clothes racks to dry the toys when painted." The set up allowed Joy and his helpers to dismantle the toys and ensure both the inside and outside had a fresh coat of paint before being reassembled. Joy's grandson, Roscoe Jr, who would have been four years old that year, still has a cast iron car from Joy's toy shop and much of the paint is still there, inside and out.

Santa Claus arrived as promised on December 13. He stopped at the high school auditorium first where he gave out gifts and talked to children who wanted to have a private conversation about their Christmas wishes. Radio station KICD was on hand for an interview with Santa and afterwards he rode off to his new workshop to prepare for his rounds on December 24. Children were allowed to come in and watch Santa at work on his toys and would always get a warm greeting and a pleasant conversation. Many may have been wondering which of those amazing toys would find their way to their home. Despite all the attention in the shop, the Spencer Times announced that the actual Christmas Eve rounds would be made "without any fanfare, but with a personal visit from 'Joy' Roberts, Spencer's real Santa Claus."

Just before Christmas, the Chamber of Commerce, the Jaycees, and the Clay County Fair Board presented Joy with a new watch in recognition of his years of public service in Spencer and the surrounding areas. It was inscribed with the words, "E. Joy Roberts, Spencer's Spirit of Christmas." Joy could certainly banter with the best, but the man of many words was humbled that night. All he could manage to mutter was, "Nothing I can say." Joy had given so much, and in 1947 the community fully embraced giving back. The Daily Reporter praised Joy in its Christmas Eve edition, saying "few communities can boast of such a citizen." Joy had spent thirty-five years as Spencer's Santa Claus and early on in his work he would probably not have considered the possibility, as the Reporter put it, that his efforts "would become more and more a part of the community legend that will live on for many years in the future."

To Joy, the work was its own reward, and at the end of each holiday season he could not wait to begin anew. He always saw Christmas as a year-round business, and the concurring headline of an article after Christmas read, "December 26 Means Time to Start Again for Spencer's Busy Santa." The photo caption reminded readers how much Joy's work had grown and how the Jaycees had stepped in to help that year. It was more than just the Jaycees, however. The whole community stepped up, and Joy enjoyed one of his most successful years ever. The skills learned and the enthusiasm generated by all involved were contagious, and in the end, would prove invaluable for the continuation of Joy's legacy. In 1948, Spencer would face something it had not known in thirty-five years...a Christmas without Joy Roberts.

Eight

꩜

It Won't Be the Same in Spencer

On October 22, 1948, the Spencer News-Herald opened its front-page article with sobering news for the community. "Christmas will come Dec. 25 as usual this year. But it won't be the same in Spencer. E. Joy Roberts died today." Most people may not have read that far. The headline would have been enough to bring sorrow to the entire community. It read, "Joy Roberts, 60, Dies Near Ogden." Joy was loved in Spencer by both children and their parents because he epitomized the "Spirit of Christmas." Suddenly, just as the holiday season was about to begin and children were anticipating the usual Christmas routine, Spencer had to gather its resources to replace what the newspapers called "a dedicated program that few cities could equal. Here it was largely a one-man job."

Joy was alone when he passed away. He had been on another business trip to Des Moines and was on his way back to Spencer. His car was found out of gear in a cornfield near Ogden, Iowa in Boone County. The medical examiners determined that Joy had suffered from a heart attack and driven through a ditch into the cornfield where his car came to rest. The article did not provide many details about his passing, and none were necessary. The Herald pointed out the obvious that Joy was one of Spencer's most loved citizens, and the people of Spencer were more interested in honoring him than mourning him. "He loved children—a reciprocal matter—and his generosity and untiring work on their behalf are a sort of Spencer legend." No one in Spencer would allow that legend to be forgotten.

After thirty-five years as Spencer's Santa Claus, Joy's funeral would be a community event regardless, but his affiliations with numerous fraternal organizations ensured there would be even more splendor than usual. He had been a member of the chamber of commerce and a "prominent Elk." He also achieved a high level of success in both the Shriners and Freemason organizations.

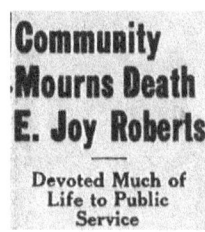

Community Mourns Death E. Joy Roberts

Devoted Much of Life to Public Service

Headline from the Spencer Times

His status in the Masonic community was impressive. He served as head of the Temple Council and the Azotus Commandery and as High Priest of Clay County Chapter No. 112 of the Royal Arch Masons. At his funeral, the Masons met at their local lodge and marched to Grace Methodist Church with a guard provided by the Knights Templar.

Reverend F.W. Ortmeyer of Grace Methodist Church officiated the funeral service. The local Nubbins quartet, also known as the Four Nubbins, sang the hymns "Abide With Me" and "Nearer My God to Thee." Joy was buried in the family plot in Riverside Cemetery near his parents and his brother, Thomas Jr. His pall bearers were longtime friends Noel Driscoll, Arthur Bjornstad, Harry Lawrence, Robert Miller, Nels Rindsig and Bob Mitchell. For several pall bearers, this tribute to their friend Joy Roberts would not be the last. Four of the six quickly changed their focus to keeping his legacy and memory alive for future generations in Spencer.

For Joy's friends and the residents of Spencer, there were three priorities to consider. How to ensure work Joy had already completed for the upcoming Christmas season could move forward uninterrupted, how to continue his work for many Christmases to come and how to ensure the memory of Joy and his contributions to Spencer and Clay County were never forgotten. The great outpouring of support Joy experienced in 1947 had been a huge boost and as a result, he had been able to complete quite a bit of work in advance. Several boxes of toys were already packed up, and many more toys were in various states of repair, so the current Christmas seemed to be off to a good start. Joy had expressed a desire to find an apprentice to take over his work in the future. His unexpected death prior to finding a successor put the continuation of his work in doubt, but there were many people committed to making it happen.

To the credit of the entire Spencer and Clay County community, the immediate priority focused on how to perpetuate the memory of Spencer's patron saint. That hope was shared by Joy's long-time friend, King Larson, in a telegram received by the family on November 25. King Larson was a band leader who performed at local fairs and met Joy through their work. "Have just learned of the passing of my fraternal brother and friend Joy Roberts. The children of Spencer have for many years been privileged to know and love him. The children of tomorrow will be denied the blessings of his warm heart. Please extend to the family my deepest and sincere sorrow and may I join his friends and the people of Spencer in mourning the loss of the 'Little Fellow,' truly a big man. I know Spencer will perpetuate in his memory his great work."

The people of Spencer were way ahead of him. On October 27, just five days after Joy's passing, the Spencer Reporter shared some of the suggestions pouring in for an appropriate tribute, "something that will suggest the type of man Joy was, and the type of things he did to become the Santa Claus of Spencer." Four suggestions had the most momentum, and three of them were not only followed up on but still exist in one form or the other to this day. The one that did not happen was the creation of a bust of Joy that would be displayed in a prominent location. Someone else suggested a plaque instead of a full bust. Joy did get a plaque placed in his honor at a local park in downtown Spencer a few years after his passing, and it is still there today.

The memorial is a beautiful bronze plaque affixed to a small boulder in a park on the property of Spencer's former Municipal Utilities building, now home to the Spencer Police Department. It reads, "In memory of Spencer's Santa Claus E. Joy Roberts, 1888-1948. Who for thirty-five years played Santa Claus to the

The E. Joy Roberts memorial plaque

needy children in this community. May his untiring efforts, his sacrifices and generosity ever be an inspiration to all to share their blessings with those less fortunate."

Many people suggested the creation of a memorial fund to ensure Joy's work would continue for many years to come. The fund began as the E. Joy Roberts Memorial Fund and has evolved over the years but never gone away. The Spencer Jaycees have carried on the tradition with their annual Tree of Joy program where they distribute toys to needy children every December. A post on their Facebook page in December 2024 referred to the Tree of Joy as one of their favorite annual projects. "Tree of Joy" is also a reference to the memorial that received the most support in 1948, a tree "of tremendous proportions" to be placed on the same site that now houses the plaque in Joy's honor. The initial fundraising in 1948 kicked off with locating and planting this Christmas tree as top priority.

Joy would have appreciated the plaque, but he was never in it for the accolades. He would be thrilled that people were still willing to give money to support needy children. As a symbol, however, many people were convinced that Joy would have loved the idea of a Christmas tree, the more brightly decorated the better. Joy Roberts and Christmas "were synonymous to everyone in the area." A supporter of the Christmas tree idea explained it. "His life was the spirit of Christmas, and lots of people might, in passing the tree during the holidays think back to this man who thought so much of other fellow's welfare than he did his own."

The idea of starting a fund to cover the costs of the memorial tree gained ground quickly. The efforts were led by Bob Mac-Dowell, who had been a generous supporter of Joy's work, having donated the new paint machine to him in 1946. MacDowell organized a committee to get the fundraising started. Four of the committee members had been pall bearers for Joy and the mayor of Spencer was also fully onboard. The committee members were Mayor Charles E. Curtis, pall bearers Noel Driscoll, Arthur Bjornstad, Harry Lawrence, and Robert Miller, along with Dean Cornwall, Dale Byrne, and Mrs. Jane King. The goal was to raise funds by soliciting individuals and various fraternal organizations to acquire the tree, light it, and hold annual children's Christmas programs nearby.

One organization had already planned to collect donations at their annual Christmas party. The Past Noble Grands Club of Rebekah, a brand of the Odd Fellows, requested that members bring gifts to their event to be turned over to the Joy Roberts Christmas Fund and handed out at Christmas. The immediate need, however, was collecting money to help find, relocate and decorate a tree prior to a planned dedication on December 7. The initial goal was to raise $1,000 and light the tree with two hundred lights, or an average of $5 per light. MacDowell pointed out that each light did not actually cost $5 but used that number as symbolic of the overall costs involved. Some businesses and individuals used that as incentive, offering to pay for an individual light with each $5 donation.

The committee anticipated that costs would be offset by donations of services and materials, and offers of trees were coming in quickly from around Spencer and other Clay County communities. William Treimer from nearby Hartley told the committee, "It would be a pleasure to furnish you with the pine to reflect the spirit of Christmas and the spirit of Joy Roberts who did so much for your good city of Spencer." For once, Spencer looked forward to cold winter weather as it would be easier to move a large tree when the soil was frozen. Without cold weather, it was possible the tree could not be relocated prior to the planned ceremony.

When the tree was selected and ready to be moved into place, several residents enthusiastically jumped in to assist. Frank Svehla from the Spencer Cartage Company offered use of a truck and driver to pick up and deliver the tree. Clarence Erickson volunteered to do all the electrical labor and Ken Herbster offered to help obtain any electrical material needed. Local organizations began to get involved, with the Business and Professional Woman's Club being one of the first to donate the cost of one of the lights to decorate the tree. The Elks Club planned several projects to raise money. The donations of cheap or free labor would ultimately lower the cost of placing and decorating the tree, and any funds saved would be used for the usual Christmas activities and toy distribution.

As soon as word went out, donations came in quickly, and not just from Spencer. Contributions poured in from the nearby towns of Mason City, Arnold's Park and Spirit Lake among others, and later donations came from as far as Denver, Colorado. MacDowell shared a letter that came with one of the donations. The writer expressed how pleased they were to help. "Dear Bob:" it read, "Just picked up the Spencer Reporter and read that contributions are being collected by you for the Joy Roberts memorial fund. I gladly send my donation. He did so much for the children of Spencer at Christmas time. It is lovely that he will still be with them again this Christmas in spirit." By November 16, the fund had reached half the goal of $1000.

As plans were being made to cover the cost of the tree, others were planning the dedication ceremony scheduled to take place on December 7 in Glen Pedersen Park near the Municipal Utilities building. The Chamber of Commerce announced during a meeting that Iowa senator Guy Gillette, a friend of Joy's, had been chosen to dedicate the memorial. At the same meeting, Vern Ewing presented a history of the Joy Roberts Christmas Fund and his ideas for carrying on the work Joy had already started that year. Joy had completed a great deal of work in advance, but more toys were needed, and a plan had to be implemented on how to distribute them. Ewing was tasked with developing the plan, along with Clarence Bittinger and Bob Miller.

On November 22, the Spencer Reporter announced that funds collected for the memorial tree were up to $715.25 and Bob Mac-Dowell said he hoped to hit the goal of $1000 in the next few days. He did not have to wait long. That evening in what the Reporter called "an unprecedented move," the Elks Club of Spencer donated $500 to the fund. They gave two reasons for the unusually large donation. Joy was a member of the club in the first place, and secondly, they had been planning a Christmas party for local children, but that event had been taken over by the Junior Chamber of Commerce, the Jaycees. The money that would have been spent on the Christmas party was passed on the Joy Roberts fund instead.

The timing of the donation was perfect as the committee organizing the fund decided to change their goal from $1,000 to $2,000. The catalyst for such an ambitious decision was the possibility that a worthy successor to Joy Roberts had been located. It had already been decided that Joy's daughter, Joyce Fertick, would deliver items Joy had already prepared for Christmas, and money from the fund would be used to cover any shortages with the purchase of new toys. Going forward, however, Joy's longtime assistant, Lee Jones, planned to take over to the best of his ability. To aid him in his endeavor, the committee raised their goal with the hope of building a workshop for Jones, just as it had for Joy several years earlier, and planned to raise funds annually for his work.

Up to that point, the committee assigned to raise and facilitate the Joy Roberts Fund had done a masterful job. With their work nearing completion and with the promise of a successor to continue Joy's work, the need for a permanent committee to manage the funds going forward became clear. The hope was to involve various clubs and organizations that had been instrumental in giving and raising funds for Joy over the years. The new committee would have one member from each of the following organizations: the Elks Lodge, the Eagles Lodge, the Moose Lodge, the Rotary Club, the Kiwanis, and the Chamber of Commerce. Joy's legacy appeared to be in good hands.

By November 26, ground conditions were looking good for transplanting the tree, and the weather appeared to be cooperating with several days of below freezing temperatures. Four days later the plans changed, but the dedication was still on. The committee decided that rather than one large tree, the display would include one 14-foot tree surrounded by five smaller trees. On November 30, holes were dug, and the large tree moved into posi-

JOY ROBERTS TREE ARRIVES

Dale Norton lifting the large
memorial tree into place
Spencer Daily Reporter

tion. There were some early problems as organizers debated how to move the tree from the truck to the hole prepared for it, but once again a local citizen came to the rescue. Dale Norton arrived with his wrecking truck and lifted the tree with considerable ease. The entire process took a little over two hours.

Preparations for the dedication ceremony were mostly complete, with everything on schedule, but more work still needed to be done for the upcoming Christmas distribution. Joyce Fertick worked hard to prepare, but it was a lot to do for someone unaccustomed to the challenge her father made look so easy at times. She would receive help, however. She wanted to include new stocking caps in the Christmas baskets but not sure where to obtain them. The Smart Shop and MacDowell's in Spencer stepped in and donated all the hats she needed.

Joy had prepared most of the toys needed that year, but they were packed away so he could organize them when all the gifts were ready. To better aid Joyce with her efforts, Bob MacDowell made an appeal for assistance in the Spencer News-Herald. He asked for six men who could spend an evening sorting and repacking toys for the upcoming deliveries. The men would "get good and dirty," but he appealed to the sense of satisfaction the work would provide. "To know that you had a part in making some little tot's eyes pop on Christmas morn is a feeling that will make you enjoy your own Christmas more and give added meaning to the holiday for you."

By December 4, the Christmas fund topped $1,500. While short of the goal, enough had been raised to get the memorial trees in place for the dedication. Everyone was invited to attend, with the understanding that the presentation would be short, lasting no more than twenty minutes. The cold weather that had allowed the trees to be transplanted in time would not be conducive to long outdoor events. The plan was to have the Spencer High School band perform a few songs followed by a prayer by Reverend Ortmeyer, and then the speech by Senator Gillette. The large tree would be lit with one hundred lights, and the five smaller trees would have sixteen lights each.

On the day of the dedication, Bob MacDowell used the Spencer Reporter to thank all those who made the occasion possible. He thanked everyone who gave to the cause regardless of the size of their donation. Individual thanks went out to Russell Smith and Mrs. A.E. Parker for assisting with placing the trees in the park and choosing the location. Dale Norton was thanked for the use of his wrecker along with the driver, Ralph Miller. Bill Woodcock selected the trees and gave advice on how best to install them. The electrical firm, Erickson and Lockey, put the lights on the trees and C.J. Hakes from the local light plant got them ready. The active fundraising campaign ended, but donations would still be accepted to get to the $2000 goal and help Lee Jones build his workshop.

GILLETTE DEDICATES MEMORIAL
Spencer Daily Reporter

Over three hundred people attended the dedication that evening despite the cold to honor Joy Roberts and witness the lighting of the trees. The cold impacted the program but not the enthusiasm. It was too cold for the band to play, so the Four Nubbins, who had performed at Joy's funeral service, stepped in to sing instead. There were no quotes from Senator Gillette's short speech, but according to the News-Herald, he "spoke briefly on what Joy Roberts and the spirit he brought to the community has meant to Spencer, and will mean thru the living evergreen memorial." The trees would be lit every evening through Christmas in honor of Joy. With the dedication complete, the community could now go about the business of preparing for Christmas, but the tributes to Joy would continue to pour in and his influence would reach even greater audiences before the holiday season ended.

On December 9, the familiar request for more toys went out through local newspapers, but this time it came from Lee Jones. Much of the work had been completed, but he could always use more toys to fill any gaps and start preparing for the following Christmas, a lesson learned from Joy who always looked ahead to next year. Lee still had his own business to run and asked those willing to donate toys to leave them at his house, whether he was there or not. He did not feel he would have enough time to pick up toys on his own. There would be plenty of help to distribute toys and Joyce Fertick had taken on that responsibility, but Lee would be the one repairing used toys going forward with any time he could muster.

During the last two weeks before Christmas, local newspapers could not get enough of the impact the story of Joy Roberts seemed to be having nationally, and regularly shared updates with their readers about new locations where his story had been reported. The Spencer Reporter sent a story out over the newswires about Joy and what he meant to Spencer. The story boasted of holiday activities that transpired in his workshop while he was alive and about the memorials in his honor after he had passed away. Sent over the United Press wires, the story found takers nationwide. Friends of people in Spencer sent clippings found in their local papers. The first clipping to arrive came from a newspaper in Dallas, Texas, and the following day a clipping was received from a local soldier stationed in Panama who found Joy's story in one of the newspapers there.

The Reporter speculated that the story was doubtless "carried in every metropolitan newspaper in the country." That would be difficult to verify, but the story certainly earned a wider audience outside of Iowa. A second story describing the dedication of the Christmas trees in memory of Joy went out on the national wires and received even more national attention. The Reporter proudly proclaimed that "Joy Roberts brought the spirit of Christmas to a lot of Spencerites in life. In death he has brought that spirit to a lot of people everywhere."

Residents of Spencer continued to get clippings or letters from out-of-town friends. Mrs. Dan Maxwell brought a clipping into the Reporter office sent to her by a friend in Mexico City. The article had appeared in the Mexico City Herald, an English language newspaper. The story also appeared in Puerto Rico and so inspired a young man there that he wrote a touching personal letter directly to Joyce Fertick saying how much it meant to him. The letter will be touched on later, but for now it is enough to say the young man enjoyed the legend of Santa Claus and told Joyce that, "Mr. Roberts had made this legend something real, alive, and unforgettable."

The newspaper articles were impressive in terms of their reach, but this was the age of radio. Any questions about the appeal of Joy's story disappeared when the story began to be told over national airwaves. The first confirmation of a radio broadcast featuring Joy's story came from Bob MacDowell, who received a Christmas card from friends in Los Angeles saying they had heard the story on a local radio broadcast on December 14 that appeared to be "pieced together from Reporter stories" ...that according to the Spencer Reporter. The really big news arrived the day before, however, when the Reporter received a special delivery air mail from Hy Gardner requesting as many clippings as they could provide about Joy Roberts and his memorial.

In 1948, Hy Gardner was a radio personality working for the Mutual Broadcasting System. He was best known for his nightly five-minute segments called Hy Gardner's Newsreel, where according to a Mutual program guide, he gave "his views of the news in anecdotal form. Gardner's beliefs are entertaining as well as informative." In his letter to the Spencer Reporter, he described his intentions. "I plan to use this feature as a Christmas story in my five-minute nightly Mutual network show. The show is broadcast out of New York at 8:55p.m. Eastern Standard Time (7:55 CST) and is probably carried by your nearest Mutual station."

Local radio station KICD usually aired the Hy Gardner Newsreel in Spencer in the evening Monday through Thursday. Gardner planned to use the story on his Christmas Eve broadcast. Christmas Eve came on a Friday night that year, but it did not take any convincing for KICD to air it. The Christmas Eve broadcast was touted as one of the highlights of Gardner's program according to the Reporter, and Joy's story provided a perfect fit. Hy Gardner wanted to tell the story of Joy Roberts to a national audience on the most appropriate of nights.

The same day Joy's story hit national airwaves, his family, his friends, and his community made sure his legacy carried on as they worked together to distribute toys and gift baskets to needy families throughout Clay County. It was another community effort. Cliff Richey donated 150 pounds of candy and Doudna's store added another one hundred pounds. Lena Roberts provided apples and peanuts for the baskets. Just a few days before Christmas, the Future Homemakers of America and the September Circle of the Congregational Church donated boxes full of presents and treats to add to the bounty going out to needy families.

When distribution of the gifts began, Joyce Fertick had no shortage of assistance. Some of the distribution began on December 23. Joyce covered Spencer, and many others assisted with deliveries to surrounding communities. The Reporter heard from Bob MacDowell that "everything is going according to schedule and that representatives from Royal, Greenville, Peterson, Everly, Dickens, Gillette Grove and other neighboring county towns have been very cooperative in picking up gifts to be distributed there." A special thanks went out to Tom Glidden who provided a truck and his time. Joy would have been exceedingly proud of his family and his community for their efforts to provide for needy children in his absence.

On December 29, Bob MacDowell did something reminiscent of what Joy himself would have done. He put another appeal in the Spencer Reporter asking for discarded toys. If people dropped the toys at his store, he would be sure to get them to the right people who could repair and refurbish them. Joy Roberts' work had now been passed on to his community and people who had the desire to carry on his legacy, and thanks to him, the example of how to do it.

Lena Roberts, Mrs. Claus, passed away on July 8, 1950. The pall bearers at her funeral included two who had provided the same service for Joy at his, Robert Miller and Noel Driscoll. John Shelmidine, who Joy had attempted to rescue from the basement of Bjornstad's store during the Spencer fire, also served as a pall bearer. The children of Joy and Lena eventually left Spencer and relocated to the West Coast where they spent the remainder of their lives and where their grandson Roscoe and his family still reside. His grandson, Dean James, joined the military where he had an honorable career, and settled in Alabama to raise his own family. Spencer was now on its own to care for their needy residents and perpetuate the memory of one of its most loved citizens.

Nine

Real, Alive, and Unforgettable

In the years that followed the passing of Joy and Lena, people in Spencer worked hard to keep Joy's legacy alive. His friends were driven to keep his memory fresh in the minds of the community and the community refused to let anyone forget what he meant to them. Many adults who could help to perpetuate his memory benefited from his goodwill when they were children and did not want to see the current generation of children get left behind or forgotten now that he was gone. Lee Jones was the first to volunteer his time to keep the toy drive active, and since then several individuals or groups stepped up to take over from the previous generous souls to distribute toys and gift baskets to underprivileged families.

Joy's family has worked to keep his legacy alive over the years, no one harder than his grandson, Dean James. Dean inherited Joy's Santa Claus suit and wore it often for public appearances during his time in the US Army and later for his own children and grandchildren. His daughters inherited the suit and have recently (and generously) passed it on to the author, who is enjoying sharing it with his own grandchild. Dean believed wholeheartedly in the message of hope his grandfather's activities brought to children and worked hard to continue that legacy.

During the 1950s and into the early 1960s, Joyce Fertick, her husband Roscoe, and son Roscoe Jr., moved often, spending time between Spencer, Sioux Falls, South Dakota and Washington DC. During those years Joyce collected clippings from local newspapers whenever they posted articles about her father and efforts to continue his tradition of giving. She kept the clippings well preserved and from them we can get a feel for the progression of those efforts.

Dean James playing Santa for his two young granddaughters
Dean James Family Collection

The first article was from 1953, written by a reporter from the Spencer Reporter who interviewed Joy in 1947 and wanted to share his story again. It began with a reminder of the sorrow that can impact needy families at Christmas. "Many a child has been spared a tear at Christmastime. Many a parent has been saved a heartbreak on Christmas Eve when E. Joy Roberts made his annual goodfellow tour..." It is easy to contemplate the sadness a child feels when they are forgotten at Christmas, but also easy to overlook the pain of

The author and his grandson Jerecho showing off Joy's Santa Claus suit and hats

parents who see that sadness and are unable to do anything about it. When Joy showed up at the home of a needy family, the relief of the parents would have been just as real as the surprise and happiness of their children.

The reporter reminisced about sitting with Joy in his insurance office, watching as he pulled a box of toys from under his desk. "You see, I have this here all the time. When I get fidgety...I just start to work at my desk." When asked where his insurance work comes in around Christmas, Joy simply stated, "It doesn't---it's forgotten." In 1953, locals were still carrying on his work. Sponsored by the Eagles Lodge and the Daily Reporter, Austin Shearer and the students in his industrial arts class, presumably at Spencer High School, were taking on the challenge of repairing old toys. Anyone wishing to donate toys could take them to Schnorr Motor Company. The E. Joy Roberts memorial fund remained open and active with a new group doing the job that Joy endlessly worked at.

In 1955, another saved article from the Spencer Reporter began by giving credit where many still felt it was due. "Needy children in Spencer will once again be assured a visit from Santa Claus this Christmas Eve, thanks to a fellow named E. Joy Roberts." The Reporter had taken on the challenge of keeping Joy's work going since his passing in 1948, along with other "interested individuals" who sponsored the E. Joy Roberts Christmas Fund. The names would change, but the commitment remained constant. When Bob Mac-Dowell stepped down after a permanent committee formed to manage the fund, Noel Driscoll took over. Driscoll had been one of Joy and Lena's pall bearers and a member of the first committee set up by MacDowell. In 1955, he stepped down and Glenn E. Scott, a public relations manager for the Spencer Publishing Company, took over as chairman of the fund.

The Spencer Daily Reporter facilitated all contributions to the fund and worked with various groups, individuals, and importantly, "old friends of Roberts." In 1954, fifty families and 150 children received toys and food baskets through the fund. In a change from 1953 when kids from the shop class were repairing donated used toys, in 1955 old toys were no longer being requested. All children benefiting from the fund were going to receive brand new toys. That change showed the success of the fund and highlighted the huge task Joy had taken on repairing so many toys. It had not been sustainable for others, and thanks to the success of the fund, it would no longer be necessary. Going forward, there would be no more mention of used and refurbished toys.

Twenty-nine families and ninety-eight children benefited from the fund that year. The committee also used money from the fund to purchase the "giant Christmas tree" in the Spencer Utilities Park. One of the original trees planted in Joy's honor in 1948, it had prospered even though the other trees had died. That lone surviving tree had to be moved to make way for a new building. Efforts were made to care for the tree in hopes it would survive, and in 1956 the bronze memorial plaque was set up next to it. By 1960, however, the remaining tree also died, leaving the plaque as the last remaining memorial in the park.

In the summer of 1956, the Spencer Reporter turned fundraising duties and management of the E. Joy Roberts Christmas Fund over to the newly created United Community Fund and its board of directors, consisting of Jack Phillips, John Greer and Glenn Scott. The fund would provide a Christmas dinner and toys for thirty families that year. Carroll's Bakery provided bread for the meal, Jersey Dairy provided milk, and toys for all children in those families under sixteen years old were provided by Sportsman's of Spencer.

The last article Joyce Fertick collected while living in Spencer was printed in December 1960. The article recalled stories about Joy's life, much of which has already been touched on, but there were a few unique anecdotes included. The writer claimed that Joy's full name was unknown, which is odd. It was Earl Joy Roberts, so either he had been coy about what the E stood for, or the reporter simply forgot. Locals had heard Joy refer to himself and E. "Joyful" Roberts on occasion, which was fitting. The reference to Joyful may have been saved for special occasions. When Joy and Lena's son, Charles, was born in 1916, the official birth records included his handwritten name as E. Joyful Roberts. A happy time indeed for the young couple.

The 1960 article is where the reference to Joy occasionally being referred to by the nickname "Joker" appeared, along with previous examples of his humor. He did not always dish out humor, however, as he occasionally found himself on the other side of a joke. During his initiation into the Shriners, he told leaders of the group that he had a fear of electricity. He would pay the price for that admission. During his first parade, a colleague managed to rig the seat of the single-seated buggy he rode in with electrical wires. During the parade, Joy would jump off the seat from time to time, when as he put it, another Shriner was "letting him have it." One thing becomes obvious when reading the article...it was written by a friend who like many others wanted to keep his memory alive. Another touching tribute twelve years after his death.

Over the decades since Joy's death, local newspapers would occasionally revisit his story at Christmas, including an article from 1983. It tells of the charitable activities of Joy and M.E. Griffith, a local banker who passed away back in 1924. Griffith bequeathed a substantial sum of money in his will to be used for the benefit of children at Christmas. The city of Spencer invested the money and still used the interest to benefit children in Spencer when the article was written nearly sixty years later. The anticipation of and final release of those funds was a constant topic in the news during the late 1920s, often in reference to finding ways to aid Joy with his own philanthropic work. In 1983, both men were still being remembered fondly.

Due to the gap in time between the 1960 and 1983 articles, the more recent was the first available in family records to highlight the Jaycees and their Tree of Joy activities. The Tree of Joy refers to a tree lit every year on Grand Avenue, formerly Main Street, in

Spencer in honor of Joy Roberts. It also refers to the annual program carried out by the Jaycees to continue his tradition of giving food and toys to needy children and their families, still aided in part by the M.E. Griffith fund in 1983. It is still active in 2025, and the physical Tree of Joy is still lit every year on Grand Avenue.

Back in 2002, an email to the Spencer Chamber of Commerce confirmed the Tree of Joy still existed and that there was a lighting ceremony at the start of the holiday season each year. The gentleman who answered the email, however, admitted he had been unaware the tree was named after an individual. It is easy to see why, as joy is a term used often around the holidays and not one typically associated with a man's name. The 1960 article touched on that dilemma. "Joy to the World' was not, over a period of many years, just a carol to be sung at Christmas time by many boys and girls. It was a time of rejoicing. There really was joy in the world for them. One man, E. Joy Roberts, was more responsible than any other person for such joy being found in some of the less fortunate homes in the Spencer community."

Nevertheless, the legacy of Joy Roberts lives on in the form of the Tree of Joy. The concern that the memory of the man has faded in Spencer even though his name is out there for all to see, if not recognized, was a significant motivation for writing this book. Joy, of course, would be less worried about his name and more thrilled with the giving that is still happening in Spencer each Christmas. That is not to say no one remembers him at all, it is just less common as the years go on. There are still those who remember from personal experience, who benefited from Joy's generosity in their youth. They are increasingly fewer in number but can show up in the most unexpected places.

In early 2025, Noah Fertick, the grandson of Roscoe Fertick Jr., graduated from college with a master's degree in the field of nutrition and dietetics. In March he started his first job as a registered dietitian at a long-term care facility in Vancouver, Washington. One of the first clients he worked with was a ninety-four-year-old gentleman who proudly claimed that he learned how to eat well growing up on a farm in Iowa. Noah, whose middle name is Spencer after the town Joy served for so many years, asked what part of Iowa. The gentleman had been raised near Spencer, and after more conversation, told Noah he had met Joy Roberts as a child and had fond memories of him. He was stunned to learn that his dietitian was Joy's great, great grandson. Noah and his family were equally floored by what a small world it truly is at times.

Joy is not someone who would be forgotten by those who benefited from his generosity. He made a lasting impact on everyone he met and especially the children who eagerly anticipated his annual visits or visited his toy shop to see their Santa Claus at work. His legacy has lived on and seems to be in good hands to continue for years to come, which would please him immensely. His story, however, should not be forgotten. It still has the power to inspire the same way it did in 1948 when so many new people heard the story following his untimely death. A wonderful example of that can be found in the letter Joyce Fertick received from the young man in Puerto Rico.

The young man was Rueben Pablon Jr. from Lajas, Puerto Rico. The portion of the letter published by the Spencer Daily Reporter on December 16, 1948, shows how much Joy's story can impact people who did not know him. "I just finished reading an article in a local paper, in which I read something in relation to your father, Joy Roberts. Although I am a very young boy I love with all my heart the persons that without personal interest practice charity. Your father will be consecrated forever in the hearts of all those who had the honor to know him. I like very much the legend of

Santa Claus, for I was born in New York from Puerto Rican parents. Mr. Roberts had made this legend be something real, alive and unforgettable."

Real, alive, and unforgettable. That is the power of Joy's story, and while his legacy is secure in Spencer, Iowa, the man behind the legacy should also be remembered. If his story can be shared with a new generation, his legacy of giving may inspire others to do as he did and start their own legacies. Ultimately, we find ourselves returning to the question posted in the first chapter...Is Santa Claus real?

Looking at the life of Joy Roberts, I go back to the same conclusion reached in that chapter. Santa Claus epitomizes the spirit of Christmas...of giving...so if the spirit of Christmas is real, so is Santa Claus. I am inclined to agree with the young boy who was questioned about what he wanted for Christmas over one hundred years ago. "Joy Roberts is Santa Claus."

Lena Roberts

We can also revisit the answer Lena Roberts gave to young Charles when asked if Santa Claus was real. "When Santa leaves behind gifts of love and affection---then folks have to admit that somebody special has been around, and you can call him Santa Claus, or Kris Kringle, or Saint Nick, or any one of a dozen names. In this case, you might call him Joy Roberts." The reality is that we all have it in us to be Santa Claus to those around us. The question is are we willing. Joy Roberts was, and he made people believe with all their hearts.

It may be best to go back to the start of this book; to the quote entitled "Share Your Fortune" that was printed in the Spencer Herald in December of 1913, Joy's first year as Santa Claus. Did he read that quote? Did it inspire him in any way? It would seem Joy had already made up his mind to take on the mission he so ably accomplished for many years. Nevertheless, the quote perfectly fits not only what he wanted to do back in 1913, but what he achieved in a lifetime of giving. Rather than repeating the quote as it first appeared, we can rephrase it in the past tense to show just how completely he embodied everything the quote hoped for.

Amid all the happiness and joys of the merry Christmas season Joy Roberts thought of those less fortunate---of those on whom the sun of plenty had failed to shine during the previous twelve months. He thought of the heartaches that were theirs on Christmas morning; he thought of the tear-stained eyes of the little children weeping because Santa Claus could not call at their homes. Most of his pleasure at Christmas was derived

Joy Roberts

from making others happy, from sharing his good fortune and sowing seeds of kindness wherever he happened to be on Christmas day. He gave everything, never trifling, to the little child to whom Christmas otherwise would mean nothing. He kept tears of sorrow from those eyes and brightened the day, and hundredfold for himself. Joy Roberts did it.

www.ingramcontent.com/pod-product-compliance
Lightning Source LLC
Chambersburg PA
CBHW070928130626

46555CB00001B/335